Awesome Art Activities Around the Year

20 Dazzling Projects With Complete How-to's That Connect to Your Curriculum and Delight All Learners

by Roberta Grobel Intrater

S C H O L A S T I C
PROFESSIONAL BOOKS

New York • Toronto • London • Auckland • Sydney
Mexico City • New Delhi • Hong Kong • Buenos Aires

ACKNOWLEDGMENTS

Testing the "recipes" for these projects in a classroom setting was an important element in preparing this guide. Working as an art consultant for Project ARTS (Arts Restoration Throughout the Schools), a New York City public-school program that promotes the idea that arts education reinforces interdisciplinary learning, provided that opportunity. I was fortunate to find two principals who enthusiastically supported the program and the concepts presented in this book. My warmest appreciation to Mary Buckley Teatum at P.S. 217 and Mary E. Bosco at P.S. 207 for welcoming me into their schools.

The art work that appears in this guide was created by 2nd- and 3rd-grade children with no previous art training. I'm grateful to them, their classroom teachers, Claudia Colombo, Nora Walsh, and Catherine Peterson at P.S. 217, and Sue Fisch and Eirena Kennedy at P.S. 207, and to my private students, Mark and Scott Chiusano, Laini Davis, Ari Rubin, and Sophia Wang, for their efforts and enthusiasm, and to their parents, who allowed them to contribute to this book.

I'm also grateful to the following people who assisted with this project: District 22 Project ARTS Coordinator Paul Kaplan; Judy Berk, Andrea Williams, and Stephen Grill at P.S. 217; A.P. Penny Moroney, Susan Vendetti, and class parents Laurie Vecchi and Rosemarie Carrozza at P.S. 207; Dr. Eric Hochberg, director of the Nature Printing Society at the Santa Barbara Museum of Natural History; Jim Low, authority on the lion-dance tradition; quilter Elaine Smith of Sew Brooklyn!; librarians Lee Regan and Jessica Merrill at the Plymouth Public Library; and Mary Jo Cullinan and Ellen Gumiran at the Brooklyn Public Library; and my good friends and colleagues: Trish Early, ceramic art instructor at Kingsborough Community College; Harvey Wang, Paul Singer, and Phil Scherer, who helped me over the computer hurdles; and Carol Kalen, Sea Cliff Elementary School teacher, for her sound advice and enthusiastic support.

Thanks also to the fine staff at Scholastic Professional Books, especially Editor-in-Chief Terry Cooper and Editorial Director Liza Charlesworth, who believed in this project and gave it the green light; editors Karen Kellaher and Chana Stiefel, who helped shape the first drafts, and Maria L. Chang, who skillfully refined the final draft and pulled everything together.

This book is dedicated to its first readers, with many thanks for their excellent suggestions and support— my mother, Estelle, my husband, Ethan, and my son, Zach, founder of UC-I See, a student-run University of Chicago art program for children, who saw the need for this guide and encouraged me to write it.

Cover credits: Emina Husejnovic (calendar); Sam Sirotnikov (leaf collage); Laini Davis (3-D neighborhood); Jocelyn Ochran (mask)

Cover design by **Norma Ortiz**
Interior design by **Holly Grundon**
Cover and interior photographs by **Roberta Grobel Intrater**
Interior illustrations by **Kathie Kelleher**

ISBN # 0-439-04498-7

Contents

Introduction

S tudying art provides cultural enrichment. In fact, there's a growing awareness that the practice and understanding of art actually enhances learning on all levels. At the very least, it increases children's observational and small motor skills. Art also teaches students to focus and think creatively, helping them to develop the analytical and problem-solving skills necessary for success in all academic subjects. And because children find art activities so much fun, it engages their interest and acts as a stimulant to the entire educational process.

But all this hasn't been reason enough to justify including art as an independent subject in most academic curriculums. The common excuse: lack of time. How can teachers squeeze art into the curriculum without cutting back on core subjects? The solution is exquisitely simple: Use art as an exciting tool to aid in the study of math, science, literature, and social studies because art integrates all of these disciplines. *Awesome Art Activities Around the Year* will show you how.

About This Book

T he first time I meet with a class, I always begin by asking, "What does an artist do?" "Paint, draw, and sculpt," students usually respond.

But artists do many other things, I point out. I ask students to look at their clothes, their chairs, their books, and the design of their room. They realize that artists also can be fashion and textile designers, industrial and graphic designers, architects, and so on.

We live in a visual world, surrounded by products created by visual artists. As professionals, these artists make design decisions every day. As consumers, we do, too. Everytime we purchase something—from a T-shirt to a new car—we are making a conscious decision about design.

As students become aware of this, their world takes on new meaning. They become more observant, more curious, and even more critical. Someone created this. How did he create it? Why did she choose those colors and shapes? Could it be done a different way? My next question is: "Before an artist begins to make something, what does he or she need?"

"Pencils, paint, clay ... a computer," most reply. But some will dig a little deeper. "An idea!" they shout. Right on target!

Observation, curiosity, critical thinking, and good ideas are the basis of any creative process. Creating a visual work of art isn't much different than creating a good story or hypothesis. It just employs different techniques and materials. This book is about showing students the meaning and relevance of art and teaching them how to develop and express their ideas in a visual way.

How to Use This Book

Each chapter represents a month of the school calendar and features two projects that relate to a theme. For example, October's theme is based on the changing colors and patterns of fall. One October project encourages students to experiment with color using painting as the technique; the other explores composition and design through collage, using leaves as inspiration for shape and line.

The projects appear in a logical developmental progression, beginning with fundamental art techniques (e.g., drawing, color mixing, cutting) and basic elements of design (e.g., line, shape, color). You can do the projects in any month, or tie them into your curriculum by changing the theme (e.g., make January's "Chinese New Year Lion Dance Mask" an October project for Halloween). You may also want to focus on a particular technique (e.g., printmaking) or apply the techniques described here to design your own projects. The choice is yours. Have fun with it!

Each art project is organized as follows:

Sessions: Estimated number of sessions to complete the project (If possible, combine two class periods to make one session.)

Curriculum Connections: Academic links for each project

Techniques: Methods used, such as printmaking, mixed media and collage

Art Objectives: Conceptual goals, such as abstract design and portraiture

Visual Vocabulary: Specific art terms related to the project

Art References: Artists, movements, or specific types of artwork to help you find visual samples and more information on the subject

Art Talk: Overview of the genre and the artist or stylistic movement that inspired each project

About This Project: A brief description of the project and its objectives

Materials: Items needed for individual projects

Before You Begin: Suggestions on how to prepare for each project

Step-by-Step Instructions: Production directions and design suggestions

Reproducible Templates: Ready-to-copy templates for some projects

Use This Book as:

- a guide for using art projects to enhance your academic curriculum.

- an introduction to art appreciation and the techniques, materials, and creative process of the visual artist.

- a guide for establishing a weekly arts program.

- an occasional foray into an exciting artistic adventure.

How to Organize an Art Program

Scheduling

Always factor in time for setup and cleanup when you're doing an art project. Too often, just when kids finally are getting into the project, it's time to clean up. Since learning to focus is one of the most important reasons for doing these projects, we recommend combining two class periods to make one session. If you're short on time, it might be better to do art projects in a more intensive way two times a month, rather than try to do them once a week for a session that's too short to be satisfying or productive. Most of the samples in this book were completed in one to three 2-period sessions. A good way to gauge the time factor is to make the project yourself. This will also help you decide if the project is right for your students and provide them with a sample they can examine.

Setting the Tone

The more background and visual samples you can provide, the more your students will get out of each project. Trips to museums, botanic gardens, aquariums, zoos—even a walk around your neighborhood—will inspire them and enrich their understanding of art and design. Your input is essential, but you also should encourage your students to do some work on their own. Encourage students to keep a small sketchbook handy to practice drawing, sketch project ideas, and jot down notes.

Storing Artwork

Provide a portfolio for each student in which he or she can store finished and unfinished artwork to protect their work and keep it organized. You can buy accordion-style envelopes or have the students make a portfolio out of two pieces of cardboard hinged with masking tape. (Collages with lots of loose pieces should be placed inside large folded sheets of newspaper before storing.)

Exhibiting the Art

After students have finished a few projects, you may want to reward their efforts with an art exhibition. Students will find it very exciting, and it will give them an incentive to continue producing quality work. It may even help generate support for art programs in your school or school district!

Basic Materials

You'll find a complete list of materials you need under each project. Here are some basic supplies that you'll need for several projects:

- Pencils, vinyl erasers, medium- and fine-line black marker pens, and colored markers (or pencils and crayons)

- Rulers (You may also want to get an 18-inch metal T-square.)

- Scissors (Five-inch precision scissors are especially useful for cutting small details or shapes out of the center of a piece of paper. The seven-inch pointy, all-purpose scissors can be used for any project.)

- Glue sticks, white glue, masking tape

- Copy paper for layouts, practice sketches, and book projects

- A ream (500 sheets) of 80-lb white 12- by 18-inch drawing paper

- Colored construction paper in two sizes: 9- by 12-inches and 12- by 18-inches (We recommend sulfite-based construction paper. It's slightly more expensive than standard construction paper, but the colors are more brilliant and don't fade. It's best to order individual colors in 50-sheet packages. Don't forget to include black and white!)

- Tracing paper

- Corrugated cardboard (heavy-duty 18-inch corrugated cardboard pizza boxes are a good source) and Styrofoam trays for reusable palettes and projects (ask your local retailers to order some for you).

- Tempera paint in red, yellow, and blue, plus black and white

- An assortment of paint brushes (Buy the best quality you can afford.)

- Containers for distributing paint and water (16-oz tin cans, baby-food jars, or yogurt cups), plus some buckets if you don't have a sink

- Newspapers for protecting surfaces; paper towels, sponges, and baby wipes for cleanup

- A smock or work shirt for each child

Basic Skills and

The first thing most teachers think about when it comes to doing art is the mess it's going to make. There's no denying that art can be messy, but don't let that deter you. Most of the mess can be controlled when students know how to handle their materials. Before beginning a project, demonstrate the technique they'll be using. Your students will learn how to produce clean work more efficiently, and you'll have your classroom back in order in no time. Following are some tips for basic techniques:

Gluing

- **WHITE GLUE:** Make two "squeegees" by cutting 1- by 4-inch rectangles out of both Styrofoam and cardboard for each child. Have students lay their artwork facedown on newspaper. Squeeze just enough glue in the center of the back of the art—too much glue will make the paper soggy and likely to rip; too little won't spread enough to cover the sheet. Use the cardboard squeegee to spread the glue from the center out, across the edges of the paper, and onto the newspaper. Lift the artwork and mount. Use the soft Styrofoam squeegee on the face of the art, always moving from the center out, to finish the job. Using squeegees prevents hands from becoming sticky. Using two different types of squeegees helps students avoid the mistake of using the gluey one on the front of their art.

  If students are mounting paper onto a stiff surface, such as cardboard, don't lift the art. Leave it facedown, lay the board on top of the art, and line it up squarely with the edges of the art. Smooth down the cardboard with your hand. Then flip it over and squeegee across the art.

- **GLUE STICKS:** To avoid gluey build-up and messy hands and artwork, twist the glue out just a bit at a time. Lay the art or collage piece facedown on the newspaper and hold it in the corner with a finger. Keep the glue stick upright and drag it across the surface in overlapping lines, past the edges, until the entire surface is covered. (Always use glue sticks for collage. When gluing lots of pieces, remind students to fold or change the newspaper to avoid laying a clean piece on a gluey spot.) Lift and press the piece onto the new surface. Cover the glue sticks when not in use.

Techniques

Cutting

As a general rule of thumb, flimsy tools make work more difficult. Good-quality pointy scissors are a good investment. Sharp sturdy scissors are essential for cutting stiff surfaces such as cardboard. Always begin by reviewing safety tips with students and warn them that scissors are very sharp. You may want to inject a note of confidence, telling them you're sure they can handle the scissors properly.

Remind students that they need to use both hands for cutting. Show them how to hold the paper firmly in one hand. Here are more tips:

● To cut freeform or circular shapes, rotate the papers as you rotate the scissors.

● To cut a shape out of a larger piece of paper or cardboard, cut roughly around the shape to release it. Then trim to the exact shape.

● To cut an irregular shape out of a stiff surface like cardboard, make some cuts into the cardboard perpendicular to the line. Cut the excess material away in small pieces along the line or just below it, and then trim. This will keep the cardboard from bending.

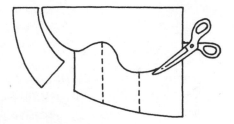

● To make an interior cutout (or open shape), like a window, place your hand in back of the paper (behind the shape) to support the paper, spread your fingers, and gently poke a hole between fingers into the center of the shape with the point of the scissors. Insert the scissors and cut a couple of diagonal lines from the center to the corners. Cut along the line connecting the corners and continue. To cut out circles and irregular shapes, poke the hole and cut a line from the center of the shape to the outline. Rotate the paper as you cut out the shape.

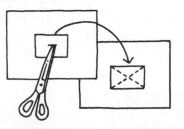

Painting

● **SETTING UP:** Push students' desks together and have them work in small groups so they can share materials. Cover the desks with newspaper. If you don't have a sink, get some buckets—a couple for clean water and an empty one to collect the used water. Fill 16-oz tin cans or small yogurt containers halfway with water and distribute them with the brushes and paint. Each child will need a Styrofoam tray or plate for a palette, some paper towels, and a smock or work shirt.

- **PAINTING:** Students can mix all the colors they'll need from the primary colors (red, yellow, and blue), plus black and white. You may want to buy the tempera paint in gallons—it's more economical. Plastic pumps will make distribution much easier. Also, have some paint stirrers on hand (tongue depressors work well).

- **USING BRUSHES:** Children have a tendency to dip their brush into the paint as far as they'll go. Explain to them that they shouldn't overload the brushes. In addition to being wasteful, pushing paint into the ferrule (metal holder) will ruin the brush. Too much paint also will make a brush harder to use and clean. Show students how to dip the brush partway into the paint, keeping most of the paint on the tip.

- **WORKING CLEAN:** Keeping colors from getting muddy is a major problem for all painters. There are several ways to avoid this (see "Exciting Experiments with Color," page 26), but the first hurdle is teaching students to clean their brushes before dipping into another color. Tell them that they have to use two hands and two tools when they paint—a paper towel and a brush. They should rinse the brush in water and blot off the excess water with the towel. I tell my students there's a rhythm to painting: dip, paint, rinse, wipe; dip, paint, rinse, wipe. I even have them sing it out loud a few times. (If the brush is overloaded with paint, students should wipe it off on newspaper first, then rinse and blot it. This will prevent the water from getting too muddy too fast.)

    Explain to students that the brush should be damp enough to carry the paint but not so wet that the color is watered down. The brush also shouldn't be so loaded with paint that it loses its shape and becomes difficult to control. Remind students that they're sharing materials, so they should be especially careful not to pollute (or mess up) the paint. All color mixing should be done on their own palettes (Styrofoam trays). It's important to keep the colors clean and separated on the palette, too. Working clean helps keep colors pure and bright. Once children understand that, they usually do their best to do it right.

Drawing

- **USING A PENCIL:** The pencil is the primary drawing tool. Make sure your students are holding their pencils correctly. Some students hold their pencils in their fist when they write or draw and push the pencil into the paper so hard it leaves indentations. Show them how to rest the pencil against their middle finger. This will allow them to draw more fluidly and give them more control over their work, and may even improve their writing habits.

Tip

To keep brushes in good condition, wash them with soap and water, blot with paper towels, and reshape the tips before putting the brushes away.

● **OUTLINE DRAWING:** All the drawing for the projects can (and should) be done in simple outline form—the style of drawing with which children are most familiar. If students are drawing a single object from life (like an apple or a shell), they can lightly sketch the basic shape and then go back and refine the outline.

Students can also use another technique called *contour drawing*, where they focus on the edges (contours) of the object and draw the object spontaneously. This will produce a very expressive line, and help develop good hand-eye coordination. Before students begin to draw, tell them to look at the object carefully, analyze its basic shape, and pay particular attention to the edges. As students draw, their eyes will move back and forth between the object and their drawing. They should try to imagine their pencil moving along all the little bumps and dents that give the object its distinctive shape.

Some children may be reluctant to draw at first. They want to do it, but they're afraid they won't get it "right." Usually, their biggest concern is that their drawings won't look real enough. Point out that many artists, including Picasso, Matisse, and Klee, admired the drawings of very young children for their directness, simplicity, and expressive qualities, and tried to achieve similar effects in their own work. Show them caricature drawings (which rely on exaggeration for effect), cartoons, and works by folk and modern artists, who intentionally work in a childlike style. This will help them understand that art doesn't have to look "real" to be good. But it does have to be well-designed.

● **FORMAT:** I once asked some of my students why they insisted on drawing so small and leaving so much blank space on the paper. "That's easy," said one third-grader. "The bigger we get, the smaller we draw."

He's right. Five-year-olds make big, free, exuberant drawings that fill the paper. As students get older and become more self-critical, their drawings start to tighten up and shrink. They tend to focus on the subject they're drawing, which they may lavish with wonderfully intricate details, but pay little attention to the overall composition— the way objects relate to one another and the surrounding space within the format.

Many students don't realize that paper actually is a design format, a blank surface on which to draw. The empty background seems like air, and air has no borders, so they'll place their drawings anywhere—objects often wind up floating in space. Explain that the edges of the paper are the borders that define the format and that the figures, objects, or shapes they place inside the format need to relate to those borders, as well as to one another and the surrounding space. Then show students how they can turn their paper to create a vertical or horizontal format.

- **LAYOUT DRAWINGS:** When students are working on a project such as a scene or still life, they should lay out all the elements of the composition first, loosely drawing the main structures, figures, or objects with simple basic shapes. This will allow them to make changes easily. Once they have everything in place, they can refine the shapes, add the details, and darken the lines by applying more pressure to the pencil.

- **THUMBNAIL SKETCHES:** Most artists make small, rough "thumbnail" sketches to lay out a composition or design. Starting with a few thumbnail sketches (in any style) will help students focus on spatial arrangements, rather than on the objects or details, and give them a chance to explore a number of ideas quickly before moving on to larger drawings.

  Thumbnail sketches should be made in a format of the same proportions as the finished artwork. The easiest way to create the format is to trace around a cardboard template that's scaled to the right size. Many projects will be done in 9- by 12-inch or 12- by 18-inch formats (the standard size of drawing and construction paper). To create a template for the 9- by 12-inch format, cut a 2 1/4- by 3-inch rectangle. For the 12- by 18-inch format, cut a 2- by 3-inch rectangle.

- **SKETCHBOOK DRAWINGS:** Sketches can be done in any style—rough lines, loose lines, outlines, scribbled lines—whatever comes naturally. Tell students there's no right or wrong way to draw; every artist has his or her own style, which makes the work unique. But remind them that they can always improve their technique. Like anything else, the more students draw, the better they'll get. Keeping a sketchbook handy will give them an incentive to do more drawing.

Creating a Collage

Collage is both a method and an art form. It's a cut-and-paste technique that involves attaching layers of relatively flat materials—paper, fabric, plastic, string, and so on—to a flat surface. Collage is also an arrangement of elements designed to express an artistic idea. All the collage projects in this book are created with cut or torn paper.

Working in collage is a great way to learn about design, because

students can add, take away, and rearrange elements until they're satisfied with the composition. Shapes can be flipped (turned upside down), flopped (turned left or right), or rotated to change their angle. Students can create multiple shapes quickly and easily to make their patterns or designs. And best of all, they can experiment freely without the pressure of getting it right the first time—nothing is permanent until it's glued down.

When creating a collage, let students select the colors they want to use. Students find this very exciting, and it gets their creative juices flowing. You may have to guide them a bit if they seem to be choosing colors that are too close in value, but for the most part, children have a knack for putting together the most surprising and wonderful color combinations.

● **ORGANIZING COLLAGE MATERIALS:**
   1. To simplify the color selection process, separate the construction paper into broad categories of warm and cool colors, and then add a third category for neutral colors and black and white. Within each category, cluster the colors together by hue and value (e.g., bright red, dark red, pink). Store the paper upright in its own box, rather than laying it in a pile on a shelf. This makes it easier to pull out a single sheet of paper and avoid wrinkling.

   2. Keep two boxes for cutoffs and scraps—one for smaller scraps and another for larger pieces. Saving scraps is economical and ecological. Equally important, the cut-off shapes often give students ideas and can contribute to a design in progress. One child's cutoff may make a perfect addition to another child's design!

   3. You'll need half or quarter sheets of newspaper for the gluing process and large folded sheets of newspaper for storing unfinished work. Slide unfinished collages inside the folded sheet carefully to keep loose pieces in place and store in a flat position. Slip a piece of cardboard under the pile to make it easier to move, or have students store the pieces in their portfolios.

● **COLLAGE TECHNIQUES:** There are two basic techniques for creating paper shapes: cutting and tearing. Each produces different edges, which create different effects. Cutting creates a sharp, graphic edge that makes a shape appear to come forward. Tearing creates a softer, more decorative edge that blends into the background. Combining shapes with different types of edges will add contrast, variety, and the illusion of depth to a two-dimensional design. The following suggestions are specific to collage:

Note

Students who haven't had much experience with scissors will need a short cutting lesson and some practice before starting a collage or any other project that requires cutting (see page 9).

1. **CUTTING SHAPES:** Have students draw the designs on drawing paper first, then cut out the shapes and use them as templates to cut the colored paper. This will help them plan their compositions and avoid wasting construction paper.

2. **TEARING SHAPES:** Draw the shape on colored paper or lightly trace around a template. Cut a larger shape around it, about one inch away from the drawing. Then hold the paper in both hands, putting both thumbs next to the pencil line and working them back and forth together, tearing the paper gently and slowly in small increments to create a soft edge.

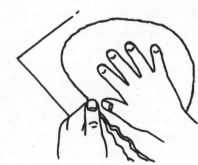

3. **CUTTING OPEN SHAPES:** Making an open (or outlined) shape is a great way to create a line and shape at the same time. First cut the shape, then poke a hole in the center and cut a parallel line that follows the form to cut out the center.

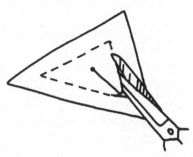

4. **TEARING OPEN SHAPES:** Cut the shape and draw a parallel line inside it. Poke a hole in the center with a scissors, cut part of the center out to get into the form, and then tear along the line with the thumbs the same way as above (Tearing Shapes).

5. **CUTTING SYMMETRICAL SHAPES:** Symmetrical shapes can be cut on one side of a fold, but this will crease the paper. To avoid that, make a template. Draw the shape, fold it in half, and cut. Then open the template, place it on a few layers of colored paper, and cut (or tear) around the full shape.

6. **CUTTING REPETITIVE SHAPES:** Here are some ways to do this efficiently:
   ● Fold the paper accordion style or in half or quarters. This is a quick way to cut a lot of small pieces, such as leaves or petals, in

one color. Draw the shape or place the template near the corner to leave room for cutting other shapes.

● Use the entire sheet. This is a quick way to produce multiple shapes in different colors. Draw or trace around the shapes on a sheet of colored paper sheet, put a few other colored sheets behind it, and cut them together. Place the shapes close to the edge of the paper to get the most out of the material.

● To create negative (cutout) and positive shapes at the same time, cut one or a few different colored sheets together. Cut a sharp line from the edge of the paper to the outline and cut the shape. You'll be left with one or a few large sheets with cut-out shapes that can be placed over a different background color to create a see-through effect. You'll also have the positive shapes. If you don't need the positive shapes, start by poking a hole in the center of each shape and cut the inside away.

● **ASSEMBLING THE COLLAGE:** In most cases, the process of design takes place as the collage is being assembled. This is the fun part. Encourage students to play with the design—move shapes around, add, remove, or change them until they're satisfied with the results. Shapes that were drawn on colored paper should be turned over before students begin to assemble the design if they don't want the pencil marks to show (erasing construction paper may lighten it). Apply the glue to the side with the markings.

● **GLUING:** Once the design is assembled, leave all the pieces in place and glue on one piece at a time using a glue stick. Glue the top pieces first and work down to the next layer. With partially overlapping shapes, put glue only on the part that overlaps. Attach them and then glue the combined shape to the next layer. Details can be glued to each piece before attaching it to the collage or added after all the pieces are glued down. Small details should be glued on as soon as they're cut.

Composition and Design

Line, shape, color, value, and texture are the basic elements of design. All these elements can be made and combined in an infinite number of ways. Think about the variety of lines—they can be thick, thin, jagged, smooth, broken, straight, curved, wavy, dotted, hard, soft; they can be colored, dark, or light; they can define a shape or create texture. Shapes can be big or small, geometric, linear or freeform, open or closed, hard-edged or ragged; they can have a variety of textures, an endless number of colors, and can range from dark to light. Design is about selecting and arranging these elements into a unified composition.

Choosing a horizontal or vertical format is the first step in most of the two-dimensional projects. Any subject can work in any format, as long as all the elements relate to each other and the surrounding space. A tall vase will work in a horizontal format if it's set on a wide table or if lines or shapes are added to the background to pull together the composition.

Understanding the interplay of space and shape is one of the most important aspects of design. Space gives the colors, shapes, and lines something to play against. Space can also function as a shape. The positive shapes (solid forms) and negative shapes (spaces around and between the positive shapes) fit together like a puzzle. Making one larger will make the other smaller and alter the overall composition.

Design elements can be used to create a mood or evoke a feeling or emotion. Verticals and horizontals add stability to a design because we associate them with stable positions, such as standing or lying down. Diagonals and jagged or pointy lines and shapes remind us of more dangerous things such as shark bites or falling, and add tension and excitement. So do jarring color combinations, contrasting darks and lights, and rough textures. Rounded or wavy lines or shapes, floating forms, softer or subtle transitions of colors, tones, and textures create a gentler feeling and more tranquil or melancholy mood.

The organization of these elements can also evoke an emotional response. The stability of symmetrically balanced designs creates a feeling of harmony and order. Asymmetrical arrangements add tension, excitement, and drama. Selective arrangements of colors, values, shapes, textures, and lines can activate a design or create a feeling of rhythm or movement. The Sea Life collage (left) is a good example. Using a big fish to create a dominant form establishes a center of interest. Setting it off to one side and placing it on a diagonal adds a feeling of movement and tension that emphasizes the drama of the narrative (the big fish gets the little guy). The black eyes and heavy black weight along the bottom, the variety and contrast of small and large shapes, the vibrating colors, and hard and soft edges move the viewer's eye around the collage and balance the asymmetrical composition. It's a dynamic and unified design.

Encourage students to experiment with design. Let them explore spatial relationships and alternative ways to create emphasis, contrast, rhythm, and balance. Then each work will be as unique as the child who made it.

Resources

Material Sources

Most of the materials used in these projects can be purchased at local art supply or stationery stores. You can also order supplies through national school art supply catalog marketers:

- Sax Arts & Crafts (800-558-6696 or **www.saxarts.com**)

- Dick Blick Art Materials (800-828-4548 or **www.dickblick.com**)

- NASCO (800-558-9595 or **www.nascofa.com**)

- TRIARCO (800-328-3360 or e-mail: **info@triarcoarts.com**)

Contact them for free catalogs and paper samples. Remember to ask about special school discounts and billing arrangements.

Visual Reference

- Many libraries have picture collections and art videos available for loan.

- The National Gallery of Art in Washington, D.C., loans slide programs, teaching packets, videocassettes, videodiscs, and films at no cost. Call (202) 842-6973, or visit their Web site at **www.nga.gov.**

- The Smithsonian Institute offers free teachers guides. Write for their Educational Resources brochure for a list of materials at: Education Office, Smithsonian American Art Museum, Smithsonian Institution, Washington, D.C. 20560-0210. Their Web site is **www.nmaa.si.edu.**

- Most museums offer similar lending programs for local school districts and useful Web sites.

- Magazines, catalogs, and travel brochures are other good sources for visual reference. Encyclopedias can provide a wealth of imagery.

- Crystal Productions has an excellent catalog, *Art Education Resources,* for purchasing books, posters, museum collections on CD-ROMs, and other audio-visual materials. Call for a catalog at (800) 255-8629 or visit **www.crystalproductions.com.**

For other online resources, go to:

- Grove Dictionary of Art at **www.groveart.com**

- The Getty Center for Education in the Arts at **www.artsednet.getty.edu**

- Voice of the Shuttle: Art and Art History Page at **vos.ucsb.edu/shuttle/art.html/**

September

Theme: *All About Us*

September is the month to meet new classmates. These projects will help students learn more about one another and their environment.

Project 1: **Flip-Book Portraits**

Draw portraits of your classmates and create a flip book of many faces.

Sessions: 1–2

Curriculum Connections: Social Studies, Science

Technique: Drawing

Art Objective: Portraiture

Visual Vocabulary: Symmetry, caricature, realistic, expression, exaggeration

Art References: Sculpture: Houdon, Rodin, Duane Hanson, African and Roman portraits; **Naturalistic Painting:** Da Vinci, Titian, Rembrandt, Ingre, Sargent, Grant Wood; **Stylized, Abstract, Mixed-Media Painting:** Van Gogh, Modigliani, Picasso, Warhol, Chuck Close, Alice Neel; **Caricature:** Honoré Daumier, Thomas Nast, David Levine, Al Hirschfeld

Art Talk

For thousands of years, people have commissioned portraits to record and preserve images of themselves, their families, or well-known personalities. These portraits bring history to life. Hairstyles, clothing, and artifacts, as well as artistic style, tell us something about the cultural, stylistic, and artistic trends of the period. Pharaohs and emperors sometimes were portrayed in a stylized or idealized way to symbolize their divine status or the strength and stability of their rule, or to present them as heroic figures. Society and court painters sometimes had to flatter their subjects. The pragmatic citizens of prosperous middle-class republics—ancient Romans, 17th-century Dutch burghers, and 18th- and 19th-century Americans—preferred realistic portraiture. But a portrait doesn't have to be an exact likeness to reveal something about the subject's character or status. Caricaturists introduced humor, using exaggeration to create amusing or satirical portrayals of celebrities and political leaders. Modern artists often interpreted their subjects in more abstract and expressive ways. Contemporary artists employ various styles, media, and techniques to make a unique statement. Successful portraits capture the essence of a personality in an insightful and original way.

About This Project

The flip book will give students an opportunity to portray their classmates in their own unique style as they take turns posing and drawing one another. Using the reproducible as a guide for feature placement, each student will draw five to eight portraits. Students will color the drawings, staple them, and cut the pages into horizontal sections. Flipping the sections will create dozens of new and amusing faces. The students will learn about symmetry and facial expression. Drawing from life will help them develop hand-eye coordination and improve their observational skills. Showing different types of portraiture will help students understand that a portrait doesn't have to look "real" to be good. In fact, the more stylized or amusing their drawings are, the more delightful their flip books will be.

Before You Begin

Make one copy of the Portrait Template for each child. Tape a template on each desk (to stay there until students have finished all their portraits). Push 6 to 8 desks together so that two students are always facing each other. Prepare a sample flip book for demonstration. Show examples of different types of portraiture.

Draw the Portraits

1. Inform students that they will be drawing portraits—pictures of their classmates' faces. Direct students' attention to the templates on their desks and explain how the templates should be used:

   - The face is symmetrical. The vertical guideline divides the face in half from left to right and should go through the middle of the nose and mouth. The eyes should be placed on either side, an equal distance away.

   - The horizontal lines divide the face into the sections that are flipped. Draw the forehead and hair in the top section of the template. Place the eyes and eyebrows in the second section. Draw the nose in the third section, and the mouth, chin, and neck in the bottom section. Ears can be placed between the second and third sections.

Materials

For each student:

- Portrait Template (page 21)
- 5 to 8 sheets copy paper
- masking tape
- pencil and eraser
- 12- by 18-inch colored construction paper
- two 1- by 12-inch construction paper strips

To share:

- markers, crayons, or colored pencils
- glue sticks
- scissors

For teacher:

- standard or long-reach stapler

Tip

If students use markers, have them put a piece of scrap paper between the drawings to prevent the colors from bleeding onto the next page.

● Remind students that the oval outline of the face is just a guide. They should draw the shape of each face the way they see it. Some faces will be round or square. The shape of the jaw and chin will vary.

2. Distribute copy paper, pencils, and erasers. Have students place a sheet of paper over the template, align it with the corners, and tape it to the desk. The template will show through the copy paper.

3. Assign students sitting on one side of the desk arrangement as "models" and students on the opposite side as "artists." Have the models make an expression they can hold for five minutes. Tell the artists to draw the models' features lightly as they shift their eyes from the model to their drawing. They should just outline the features and not fill in details with the pencil. They'll color everything later with markers or crayons. Let students draw for five minutes. Then have the students switch roles.

4. After students finish their first drawing, remove it and tape a new sheet of paper over the template. Have students move one seat to their left so that each child faces a different classmate.

5. Repeat steps 3–4 until each student has done at least five drawings. When students have finished their pencil sketches, they can remove the templates and start coloring.

Make the Flip Book

1. Give each student a 12- by 18-inch piece of colored construction paper for a cover and matching binding strips. Arrange the drawings in the order students want them to appear, putting aside their favorite drawing (this will be used as the cover portrait.) Put the template on top of the drawings, and staple the pages between the binding strips.

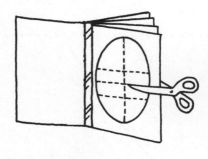

2. Have students fold the cover sheet in half. Place the bound drawings inside, centered from top to bottom. Staple the top and bottom of the binding strips to the back cover. Have students cut out the cover portrait and glue it to the cover. Add a title and the student's name.

3. Have students fold the pages back against the binding, one at a time, scoring each page sharply with their fingernail. Then press all the pages back into place. Cut all the pages together along the horizontal guidelines up to the binding. (With younger students, you may want to do this step yourself.) Then pull or cut the template away from the binding. Flip the pages to create dozens of different faces!

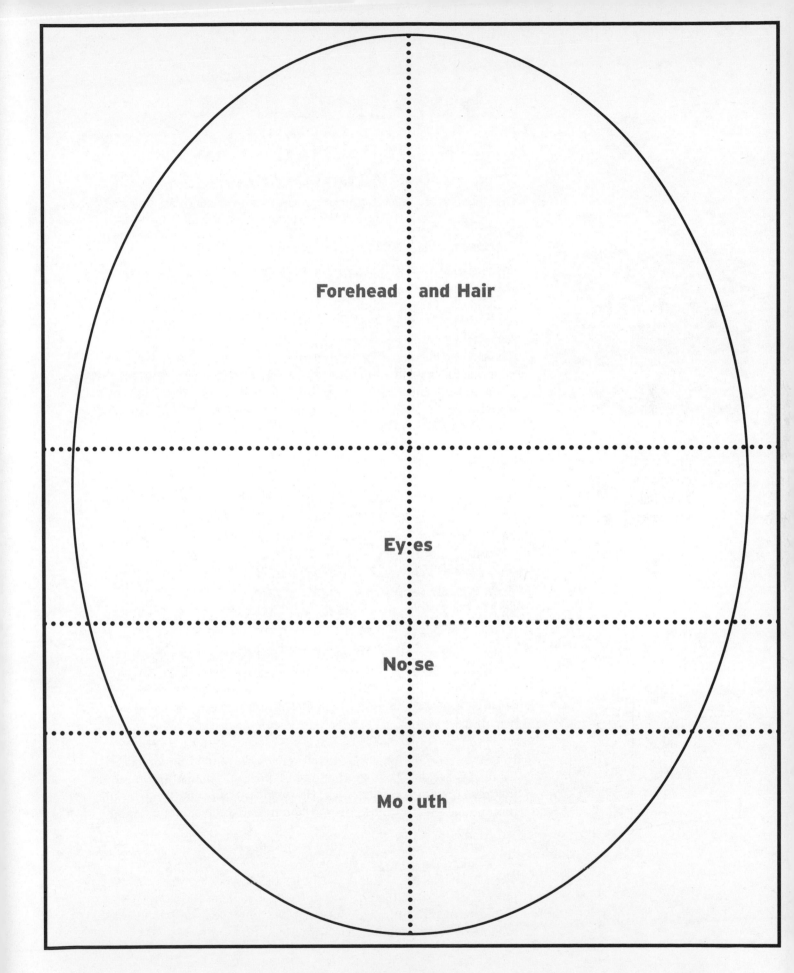

Forehead   and Hair

Eyes

Nose

Mouth

Portrait Template

September

Project 2: **3-D Portrait of My Neighborhood**

Create a colorful illustration of a local environment with pop-out figures.

Sessions: 3–4

Curriculum Connection: Social Studies

Techniques: Colored drawing, collage

Art Objectives: Illustration, composition

Visual Vocabulary: Landscape, "view," foreground, middle ground, background

Art References: Genre Scenes: medieval *Books of Hours,* Bruegel, American folk art painting, Persian & Indian miniature painting; **Views:** Canaletto, Japanese *ukiyo-e* woodblock prints (Hiroshige, Hokusai, and others), Currier & Ives prints; **3-D Construction:** Red Grooms, James Rizzi, John Suchy, Charles Fazzino

Art Talk

Scenes of everyday life often are the subjects of popular art—art made for and about ordinary people. The first major artist to develop this theme was Pieter Bruegel the Elder. His paintings and prints of Flemish peasants at work and play are filled with humor and intimate details. By skillfully integrating figures, landscape, and architecture, Bruegel created a vivid portrait of 16th-century village life. During the 18th and 19th centuries, "views" of city, town, and country sites became popular in Europe, Japan, and the U.S. While some are straightforward recordings of architecture and location, the best works capture the flavor of a particular time and place with lively portrayals of people engaged in the activities of daily life.

A few contemporary American artists have continued to explore this theme with a type of artwork called *3-D construction graphics.* Many of these whimsical works illustrate famous cities and environments of popular culture, such as sports arenas and amusement parks. Cluttered with details and done in a colorful childlike or cartoonish style, they're essentially three-dimensional collages made with two duplicate prints—one for the background and one for the pop-outs. The pop-outs are glued to the background at varying levels to create the 3-D effect.

About This Project

One of this project's primary goals is to make students more aware of their everyday environment. Using sketches or photographs for reference, students will create an illustration of their neighborhood that captures the distinctive features of the landscape, architecture, and activities.

Their scene can be a panoramic view or can focus on a small area. Students will duplicate the figures they want to pop out by tracing and transferring them to another sheet of paper. Then they'll color the drawings, mount the original illustration on cardboard, and attach the duplicate figures with pieces of Styrofoam to make the 3-D pop-outs. You can hang the completed projects individually, or link the finished constructions together to make a class mural.

Before You Begin

Show your class some examples of this theme and discuss the project. Take them on a sketch/photo tour of some local sights (e.g., a playground, amusement park, or shopping mall) or have them do this as a homework assignment. Remind students that the more details they add to their scenes, the more exciting their 3-D illustrations will be.

Draw the Scene

1. On copy paper, have students make a few thumbnail sketches to lay out their compositions. Encourage them to try both horizontal and vertical formats. One way to organize the space is to divide the format into three sections: the foreground *(bottom)*, middle ground, and background *(top)*. The size of each section will be determined by what the students want to dominate the scene. For example, to emphasize the sky or mountains in the background, make the top section larger. Students can draw shapes and figures between the lines or over them, overlapping the sections. Remind students to think about the overall composition. The forms should relate to one another, the surrounding space, and the borders of the paper. Vary the shapes and sizes to keep the scene interesting.

2. Once students have chosen a layout, they can draw their full-size illustration on a sheet of drawing paper. Have them make their drawings in outline form. Tell them not to add color or details, such as facial features or windows, yet.

Materials

For each student:

- pencil
- eraser
- copy or scrap paper
- two pieces of drawing paper (9- by 12-inch or 12- by 18-inch)
- tracing paper (same size)
- cardboard (same size)
- fine-tip black marker or crayon
- scissors
- newspaper
- ruler

To share:

- colored markers, pencils, crayons, or paint
- 12-by 18-inch colored construction paper
- Styrofoam trays or cardboard
- white glue and cardboard squeegees or glue sticks

Duplicate Elements for the Project

1. From their drawings, have students select the elements (buildings, trees, people, etc.) they want to pop out and trace them on tracing paper. They should make one tracing for group pop-outs and one tracing for each individual pop-out.

2. In the next step, students will transfer their tracings to the second sheet of drawing paper. First, have them turn over the tracing paper and place it on scrap paper. Using the edge (not tip) of the pencil, press down and rub heavy solid lines (about 1/4 inch) behind the lines of the drawings or fill in the whole space. In effect, students will be creating their own carbon paper.

3. Place the tracing paper drawing right-side up on the second sheet of drawing paper. To transfer the tracing, retrace all the lines with a sharp pencil. Have students press hard to make a good transfer.

Finish the Drawings

1. Have students fill in the details on their original drawings but only on the things that are *not* going to be popped out. Then, have them draw all the details on their pop-out figures.

2. Have students erase unnecessary lines and color the illustration and pop-out figures with markers, crayons, or paint. They can color over the figures on the illustration that are going to be covered by the pop-outs. They can also use colored paper to cover large shapes or background areas. Make a template of the shape on tracing paper, then cut out the shape from colored paper and glue the shape in place.

3. Outline everything, including details, with a thin black marker, sharp black crayon, or pencil.

Assemble the 3-D Construction

1. Have students glue the background drawing to a cardboard backing. (See Gluing, page 8.)

2. Have students cut out the pop-out figures. If tiny spaces (such as the space between branches) are too difficult to trim, have them cut around the entire shape and fill it in with the background color once the shape is glued down, or leave as is.

3. Tell students to arrange all the pop-outs on their drawings. Encourage them to analyze their illustration and consider things, such as: Is the sky too empty? Are the buildings too close in size and shape? Should there be more people, animals, or cars, or should they be larger? Do the colors of the pop-outs look good against the background? Students can change, add, or enlarge the figures by making new pop-out drawings.

4. To make the figures pop out, have students cut Styrofoam backings. The pieces can be simple rectangles. The backings should be large enough to support the pop-outs but small enough not to show. Varying the number of layers of Styrofoam backing will make things pop out at different levels.

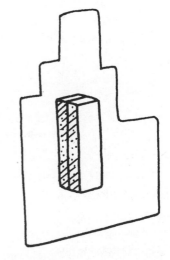

5. Glue the Styrofoam to the back of each pop-out with a drop of white glue. Then glue the pop-out to the drawing.

October

Theme: *Nature's Colors, Shapes, and Lines*
Autumn's changing colors and falling leaves inspired these October projects, which focus on color and design.

Project 1: Exciting Experiments With Color

Learn the basics of color theory, color mixing, and painting techniques.

Sessions: 1–3

Curriculum Connection: Science

Techniques: Painting, color mixing

Art Objectives: Color theory, color mixing

Visual Vocabulary: Primary, secondary, intermediate, warm, cool, complementary, and neutral colors; hue, value, shade, tint, perception

Art References: Movements and Techniques: tonalists (e.g., Rembrandt), fauves (Matisse), impressionists (Monet), pointilists (Seurat), abstract expressionists (Mondrian); medieval illuminated manuscript painting; Islamic and Indian miniatures; **Folk art paintings:** Japanese *ukiyo-e* woodcuts, Navajo blankets, Oriental carpets

Art Talk

Color is relative. You can't accurately describe a color without referring to something specific. For instance, is red the color of a fire engine, a cherry, or a brick? All these objects are red, but they vary in intensity and tonal value (degree of darkness or lightness) because of the way the objects reflect white light. Various factors, such as weather, lighting, and the atmosphere, can affect the appearance of a color. Colors look duller in shadow and on overcast days. They look warmer under tungsten lights and cooler under fluorescent lights. They seem less intense when seen from a distance. Context is another important factor. A color will look most vibrant next to its complementary color (e.g., red next to green). The same red will look darker next to white and lighter next to black. The color doesn't change but the way we perceive it does.

Artists understand the way colors interact under different conditions and the way people react to their sensory qualities. They use color to create illusions of form and depth, establish a mood, evoke an emotional response, create impact, or lead the viewer's eye around their work. In fact, color is often the defining factor in identifying the work of a particular artist, artistic movement, or cultural style.

About This Project

This project will give students a chance to experiment with color mixing and learn about the different ways colors interact to create different effects. Watch students' excitement as they create all the colors of the rainbow from the three primary colors (red, yellow, and blue), plus black and white. Using the three reproducibles, students will learn how to mix the primary colors to create secondary and intermediate colors (Color Wheel), create neutral colors by mixing complementary colors (Complementary and Neutral Colors Chart), and change the tonality of a color by adding black or white (Values Chart). The color experiments will help students develop the skills and techniques they'll need as they move on to more complex projects.

Before You Begin

Display works by various artists. Have students describe how the different artists use color. Introduce the Color Wheel (show your sample) and discuss primary, secondary, intermediate, and warm and cool colors. Demonstrate some color mixing and painting techniques: Mix red and blue to make violet, then lighten it to lavender by adding some white, or mix red and white to make pink.

Move desks together so students can work in groups and share materials. Cover the desks with newspapers. Distribute painting materials. Each student should have at least two sheets of paper towel, one brush, a palette (Styrofoam tray), scrap paper, and the appropriate chart.

Make a Color Wheel

1. Have students trim and glue the Color Wheel reproducible to the paper or Styrofoam plate.

2. Tell students that all paint should be mixed on the palette. Put about two teaspoons of each primary color on to the palettes arranged like the points of a triangle, as shown.

3. Explain that *primary colors*—red, yellow, and blue—are colors that cannot be made from other colors, but can be mixed to make all other colors.

Materials

For each student:

- Color Wheel (page 30)
- Complementary and Neutral Colors Chart (page 31)
- Values Chart (page 32)
- paper or Styrofoam plate
- scissors
- glue
- scrap paper
- 9- by 12-inch Styrofoam tray (palette)
- paintbrush
- paper towels

To share:

- Red, blue, yellow, black, and white tempera paint
- paint and water containers (ice trays, Styrofoam egg cartons, etc.)
- newspaper

For teacher:

- sample Color Wheel (already colored)

Tip

When mixing paint, always begin with the lightest color and add the darker color in small increments.

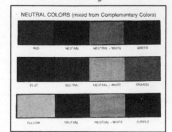

4. Have students paint the color yellow on the appropriate circle on their wheels. Then, paint the other primary colors. (Remind them to clean their brushes between colors.)

5. Next, point out the colors orange, green, and violet on the wheel. Explain that these are *secondary colors* which are made by mixing two primary colors together. For example, orange, which lies between red and yellow in the wheel, is made up of red and yellow.

6. To make orange, have students take about half of the yellow and place it on the palette between the red and yellow. Then have them mix in small amounts of red until they get a true orange, like the fruit, and paint it on the wheel between red and yellow. Have students repeat this step to make green (from yellow and blue) and violet (from blue and red).

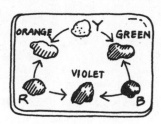

7. Mixing a secondary color with one of its primary colors produces an *intermediate* (or *tertiary*) *color*. For example, adding more red to orange will create red-orange, while adding more yellow to orange will produce yellow-orange. Have students mix different proportions of each color to create the intermediate colors on their wheels.

8. Point out that the diagonal line on the wheel divides the colors into warm and cool colors. Explain that the colors in each group are often called *harmonious colors* because they relate well to one another.

Create Complementary and Neutral Colors

1. Give each child a copy of the Complementary and Neutral Colors Chart and a clean palette. Set up palettes with the primary colors in a triangle and white in a corner.

2. Explain to students that *complementary colors*, such as red and green, sit on opposite sides of the color wheel. Remind them that red is a primary color and that green is a secondary color made from the other two primary colors, blue and yellow. When complementary colors are next to each other, they both look more colorful or intense. But when complementary colors are mixed, they neutralize each other and produce brownish or grayish colors that have little or no intensity. Artists use *neutral colors* to create different effects, such as making warm or cool shadows.

3. Have students paint the primary colors on their charts. Remind them to rinse and wipe their brushes between colors.

4. Have students mix the secondary colors between the primary colors on their palettes, then paint each secondary color on their charts.

5. Next, have them mix the complementary colors (e.g., red and green) in the center of the palette to make a neutral color and paint it on the chart. Then, have students add some white to the mixture and paint it on the chart. Rinse the brush and repeat with the other complementary colors (yellow and purple, blue and orange).

Explore Value (Darks and Lights)

1. Give each student a copy of the Values Chart reproducible and a clean palette. Set up palettes with black, white, red, and blue paint.

2. Explain to students that *value* is the amount of darkness or lightness in a color. You can change the value of a full-strength color by adding white to make it lighter or adding black to make it darker. Mixing different amounts of black and white paint will create different shades of gray. (These grays aren't as colorful as the neutral grays made from complementary colors.) Adding black to a color makes a *shade*, while adding white makes a *tint*.

3. Have students paint white on the top bar of their charts or leave the white box unpainted. Add a tiny amount of black to the white on the palette to mix the lightest gray and paint it on the chart. Tell them to keep adding black to the mixture in small increments to create darker shades of gray and fill in the rest of the bar.

4. Have them fill in the Tint and Shade bars at the center and bottom of their charts. Start by painting red in the center box. Add a tiny amount of color to the white to make a light tint and paint it on the left box of the chart. Add more color to make the darker tints. Have students clean their brushes.

5. Next, have students add a tiny amount of black to the red to make a slightly darker shade and paint it in the box to the right side of the color. Add more black to make the darker shade.

6. Repeat steps 4–5 using blue on the bottom bar.

Note

Neutral colors are very useful but also are easy to make by mistake. Bright colors can turn muddy when too many colors are mixed together—this happens when you mix colors with a brush that hasn't been rinsed. Working on this chart will help students understand why they need to rinse their brushes to keep their colors pure.

Color Wheel

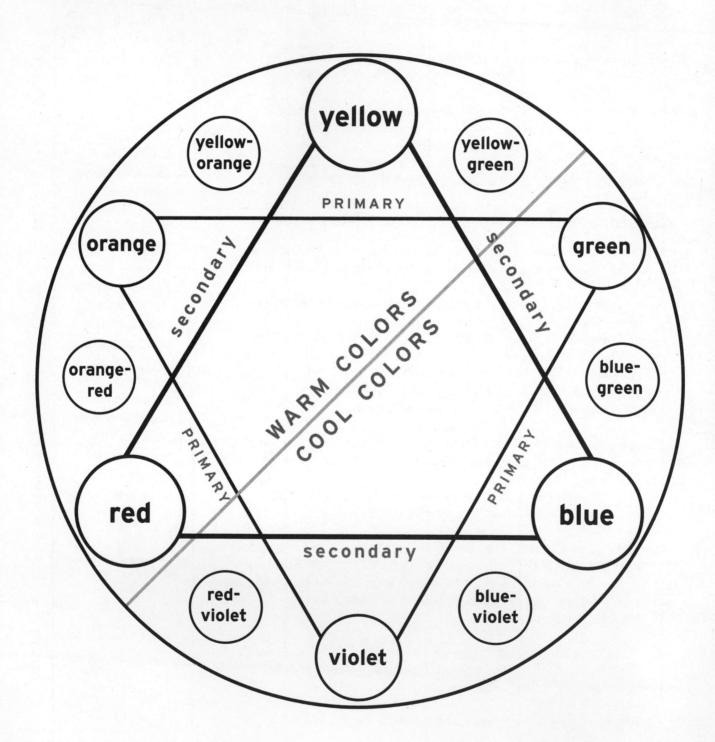

Complementary and Neutral Colors

	Neutral	Neutral + White	Green
Red			

	Neutral	Neutral + White	Orange
Blue			

	Neutral	Neutral + White	Violet
Yellow			

Values *(Lights and Darks)*

White	Light Gray	Medium Gray	Dark Gray	Black

Tints (lighter colors)		Red		Shades (darker colors)

Tints (lighter colors)		Blue		Shades (darker colors)

September

Flip-Book Portraits
COVER: *ASHAN LOUISNE*
INSIDE: *COMPOSITE*

3-D Portrait of My Neighborhood

BY *LAINI DAVIS*

October

Color Wheel

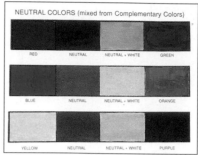

NEUTRAL COLORS (mixed from Complementary Colors)

RED	NEUTRAL	NEUTRAL + WHITE	GREEN
BLUE	NEUTRAL	NEUTRAL + WHITE	ORANGE
YELLOW	NEUTRAL	NEUTRAL + WHITE	PURPLE

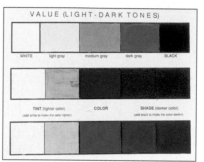

VALUE (LIGHT-DARK TONES)

WHITE	light gray	medium gray	dark gray	BLACK

TINT (lighter color)	COLOR	SHADE (darker color)
(add white to make the color lighten)		(add black to make the color darken)

Leaf Design Collage

BY *Theresa Opoku-Mensah*

Leaf Design Collage

BY *Tiffany K. Wong*

November

Thanksgiving Food Print Mural
BY MARK AND SCOTT CHIUSANO, LAINI DAVIS,
ARI RUBIN, AND SOHPIA WANG

American Indian Pottery
BY SOPHIA WANG (LEFT) AND ARI RUBIN

December

Gift Box
BY ARI RUBIN

Symbol Calendar
BY AYANIA WELLINGTON

January

Chinese Lion Dance Festival Mask

Blue mask by John De Jesus
Orange mask by Sherrihan Attia

Zodiac Animal Seals

by Mark Chiusano

February

Flag Design

BY AHMED JAVED (CLOCK), ASHLEY PYLE (HEARTS), ARIFUL HOQUE (SYMBOLS), LESLY VERTILUS (BUS), RICHARD NIEDZIELSKI (BEE), ALEEM AZAM (STRIPES), CINDIE LUU (CHECKERBOARD), VALERIY PODOLSKIY (TRIANGLE)

Block-Style Quilt Design

THREE-COLOR QUILT BY MINGO ALMODOVAR
TWO-COLOR QUILT BY WILBERTO LASALLE JR.

March

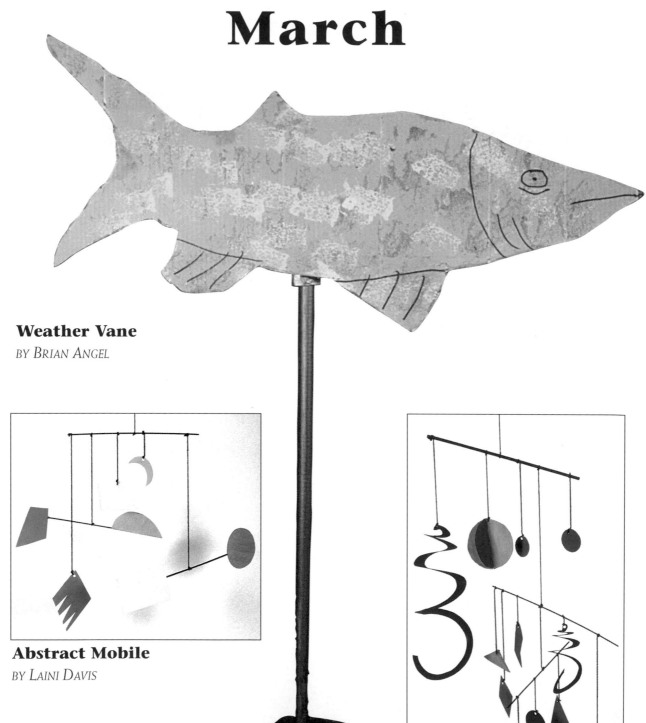

Weather Vane

BY *BRIAN ANGEL*

Abstract Mobile

BY *LAINI DAVIS*

Abstract Mobile

BY *MARK CHIUSANO*

April

Sea-Life Collage

BY MATTHEW FONG

Bug Design Prints

ENGRAVED PRINTS (LEFT) BY OLIVIA O'HARA

RAISED PRINTS BY C.J. MANGINO, STEVEN SANTIMAURO, AARON PALMER, OLIVIA O'HARA, AND DANIELLE GAUSER

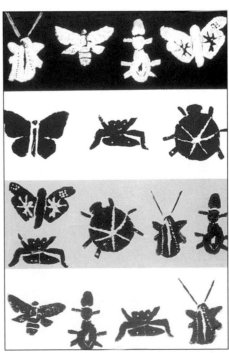

May

Still Life
BY RICCO-NOEL MACHADO

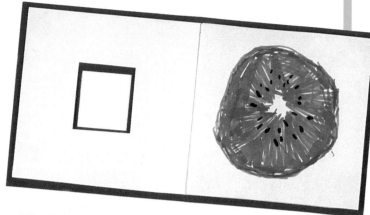

Guess What? Nature Book
BY DONALD JEUNE

June

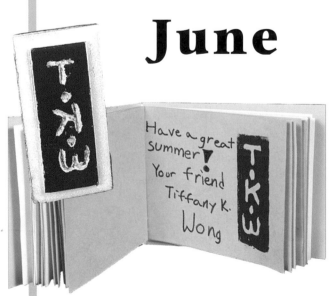

Autograph Album
BY TIFFANY K. WONG

Fun-in-the-Sun Postcard Puzzles
BY ARI RUBIN

October

Project 2: **Leaf-Design Collage**

Create an abstract design or repetitive pattern using leaves as a design reference.

Sessions: 2–3

Curriculum Connections: Science, Nature

Technique: Collage

Art Objectives: Design, composition

Visual Vocabulary: Collage, pattern, repetitive, abstract, decorative, crop, overlap, dominant, grid, symmetrical, asymmetrical, shapes (closed, open, regular, irregular, organic, geometric, linear)

Art References: Cut-paper Collage: Henri Matisse, Louise Nevelson, Arthur Dove; **Children's Book Illustrators:** Ed Young, David Wisniewski; appliqué quilt design

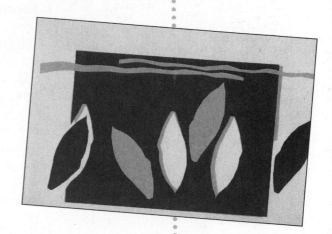

Art Talk

Picasso, the first major artist to incorporate textured materials in his paintings, often is credited with "inventing" collage. But collage and collage techniques were used long before the 20th century. Elegant paper collages were used to illustrate books in 12th-century Japan. Découpage—the popular craft of decorating objects with cut-and-pasted printed images and patterned materials—originated in 17th-century France. Picasso and his colleague, Georges Braque, who created all kinds of mixed-media collages, legitimized collage as a fine-art form. But it was Henri Matisse who created the type of cut-paper collage the students will be using for all the collage projects in this book. Matisse's collages are made entirely from colored paper cut into simple stylized figures and shapes. Matisse arranged them in abstract compositions that emphasize bold color, rhythmic line, and form. Expressive, exuberant, and playful, they have a childlike quality that's immediately appealing.

Like other modern artists, including Jean Arp, Joan Miró, and Alexander Calder, Matisse was inspired by the organic forms found in nature. Abstract leaves, seaweed, palm trees, and flowers appear as recurrent motifs in his collages.

Materials

For each student:

- pencil
- scissors

To share:

- leaves of different shapes and sizes
- 9- by 12-inch and 12- by 18-inch colored construction paper
- glue sticks
- hole punch
- newspaper

About This Project

This project is a wonderful introduction to design. The wide variety of leaf forms will provide an instant vocabulary of basic and irregular shapes and various types of lines (based on the veins, leafstalks, and edges). Students will collect leaves in different shapes and sizes. Instead of gluing the leaves to paper, they'll use the leaves as templates and cut the shapes out of colored paper. They can trace around the edges or cut the shapes into more abstract or geometric forms and arrange them into an abstract composition or pattern. They don't have to copy the colors of the leaves or even suggest a fall color scheme. The object is not to create a realistic piece of work but to use lines, shapes, and colors in an imaginative way. This is a good project to do in conjunction with a science unit on plants. Drawing will familiarize the kids with the structure of a leaf, its parts, and their functions.

Before You Begin

Take students on a nature walk to collect leaves of different shapes and sizes, or assign this activity as homework. They also can sketch or collect pictures for reference. Discuss various leaf forms. Fresh leaves should be used immediately. Otherwise, have students dry the leaves by spreading them between two or three layers of newspaper. Press the layers with books. For best results, change the paper for the first few days. The leaves will dry thoroughly in a week. Read and discuss Format (page 11), Collage (page 12), and Composition (page 16).

Draw and Cut the Shapes

1. Have students choose a color for the background and up to three colors for the shapes. Working with a limited palette will help simplify the design.

2. Students can work with one leaf, one type of leaf in different sizes, or a few different types of leaves and sizes. They can
    - trace around the leaf's edges and re-create the exact shape.
    - reduce the leaf to a simple geometric shape.
    - exaggerate, distort, or elongate the leaf's form and turn it into an abstract irregular shape.

3. Show students how to
- cut and tear the paper.

- create open, repetitive, and negative and positive shapes.

- create lines (good for suggesting stems and vines) by overlaying thin strips of colored paper on top of the shape or by cutting into or separating the shape.

Compose the Design

1. Discuss the design format and composition. Remind students to pay careful attention to the spaces around and between the shapes. Though most leaves are symmetrical, slight variations along the edges make each leaf distinct. Jagged, wavy, or smooth edges will convey different feelings in a design. Students can also exaggerate these qualities to make the design more interesting or dramatic. They can also
- use torn and cut shapes together.

- combine open (outline) shapes and solid shapes.

- combine negative and positive shapes.

- shift layers of negative shapes to create colorful edges along the openings.

- add colorful details by cutting into the shapes or adding color on top.

- overlap shapes, crop them (cut them off) at the borders, use repetitive shapes, make one shape dominant in size or color, and so on.

- create a repetitive pattern by using one leaf form in different colors or values.

- use one leaf shape in different sizes and create an alternating pattern.

2. After students have assembled their designs, have them leave all the pieces in place and glue from the top layer down. (See Gluing, page 8.)

Tip

To avoid having pencil marks show, students should turn their shapes over before they start assembling the design.

November

Theme: *Pilgrim and Native American Culture*

Expand the discussion of Pilgrims and Native Americans by learning more about their cultures. Explore the foods they ate and the art of Indian pottery.

Project 1: **Thanksgiving Food-Print Mural**

Create a food-print mural collage related to Thanksgiving.

Sessions: 1–2

Curriculum Connections: Social Studies, Nature

Techniques: Relief printing, collage

Art Objectives: Printmaking, design

Visual Vocabulary: Nature prints, rubbings, *gyotaku* (fish impressions)

Art References: Nature prints, *gyotaku*, Matisse still-life collages;
Historical Information: Plimoth Plantation **www.plimoth.org**

Art Talk

Nature printing is a relief printing process; it's the same process used to print woodcuts, linoleum cuts, and rubber stamps. Instead of printing from a carved raised surface, the object itself (e.g., vegetable, fruit, shell, or feather) is inked and printed. The print is an exact record of the size and shape of the object and most (if not all) of its surface details.

People have been making nature prints for thousands of years. Grass and plant prints dating back 10,000 years have been found in caves in Australia. The diaries and notebooks of European herbalists and physicians often contained plant prints, which were used for scientific studies. Leonardo da Vinci was known to have created plant prints with paint. Native Americans simply transferred natural pigments by pounding leaves, flowers, and stones. Inked impressions of fossils are a form of nature printing. In fact, so are fingerprints! *Gyotaku* (fish impressions) are one of the most popular forms of nature printing. Orginally used by Japanese fishermen to record their daily catch, *gyotaku* are now made by artists all over the world.

Contemporary artists use a variety of techniques and materials to transfer the image and create different effects.

About This Project

Students will make prints of different foods related to Thanksgiving using tempera paint and newsprint or construction paper. Then they'll cut out the prints and use them to make a collage mural. The mural can be based on the foods we eat for Thanksgiving; on the 17th-century diet of the Pilgrims and Wampanoag Indians; or on the foods served at the first Thanksgiving feast.

Have students make multiple prints of each food item. In addition to using the prints for the mural, students can use them to make their own collages or an illustrated book about the holiday.

Before You Begin

Decide on a theme for the mural. If you choose a historic theme, have students do some research. Make a list of the foods the class will use and ask students to bring them to school. Prepare different areas for paper distribution, painting the objects, printing, drying the prints (you can use a clothesline), and rinsing objects, hands, and brushes.

Divide the class into small groups of 4 to 6 students. Have students push their desks together and cover them with newspaper. Give each group an extra pile of newspaper (students should change the paper every time they paint and print an object). Wash and dry all objects before painting. Some foods, such as onions, squash, apples, and potatoes, will make better prints if you cut them in half.

Print the Objects

1. Have each group select objects that will be printed in the same or similar color (e.g., carrots, pumpkins, sweet potatoes) and mix the paint. (NOTE: Tell students that they don't have to use realistic colors. They can choose imaginative colors and create a more abstract design.)

2. Invite students to select their own paper for printing. Let them experiment with different colors. For example, corn prints stand out well on black paper, which emphasizes the texture of the kernels.

Materials

To share:

- food items for printing
- tempera paint
- 1/2- to 1-inch flat or foam brushes
- shallow tins or bowls for paint
- mixing sticks
- water tins
- white and colored construction paper or newsprint
- scissors
- masking tape
- glue sticks (or white glue and squeegees)
- newspaper
- paper towels
- water

For teacher:

- knife for cutting foods
- extra-large construction or mural paper
- clothesline and clothespins (optional)

Tip

Flat, dense objects that are easy to hold, such as cross-sectioned potatoes and squash, also can be printed by stamping them onto the paper. Students can print a few objects on one sheet.

Tip

Thinner paint is ideal for objects with delicate textures, such as fish, cornhusks, or feathers. Use thicker paint for smooth, dense objects, including those that are going to be stamped, such as squash or potatoes.

3. Have students place an object on a clean piece of newspaper and coat it with paint. They can coat different parts of the object with different colors (e.g., paint the corn kernels yellow, the husk green, etc.). Then, move the painted object to a clean piece of newspaper.

4. Next, have students carefully place their paper over the object. Remind them not to move anything once the paper is in position to avoid making a blurred impression. Have students rub the paper with their hands and fingertips, molding it around the painted surface. The paper may wrinkle a bit but will straighten out once it's glued to the mural. Peel off the paper carefully and place the print in the drying area.

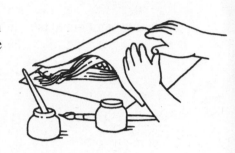

5. To make additional prints, simply have students repaint the object and print it again. After a few prints, dried paint may clog the object's surface. To restore its texture or change colors, have students rinse off the paint and dry the object before repainting. Remind students to change the newspaper for every print.

Make the Mural Collage

1. As a class, decide on the mural's design before students cut out their prints. They can design it like a patchwork quilt, made of regular and repeating geometric shapes, or they can create a mural that has a more random and abstract design. Multiple prints of small items, such as shells or string beans, can create an interesting border.

2. Students can cut the prints in different ways to make the collage:
- Silhouette the shapes by cutting along the contour of the objects.
- Cut or tear a geometric or freeform shape around the image.

3. Have students arrange the shapes on the mural paper. They can either spread the mural paper on the floor (put newspaper under it to keep it clean) or tack the mural paper to the wall. Have students put a small loop of masking tape on the back of each cutout to hold it in place while they arrange the collage design.

4. When they have finished their design, have students permanently attach the pieces with glue sticks or white glue (see page 8).

November

Project 2: **North American Indian Pottery**

Make a pot out of coiled clay and decorate it with traditional American Indian designs.

Sessions: 2

Curriculum Connection: Social Studies

Techniques: Painting, incising

Art Objective: Pottery

Visual Vocabulary: Hand-built, coil, incise, impress, motif, geometric, abstract, stylized, pot anatomy (base, shoulder, neck, rim)

Art References: Pueblo Pottery: Prehistoric Mimbres, Sikyati; **Modern Masters:** Lucy M. Lewis (Acoma), Fannie Nampeyo (Hopi), Margaret Tafoya (Santa Clara), Maria and Lucian Martinez (San Idelfonso)

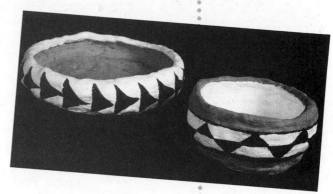

Art Talk

Native Americans have been making pottery for thousands of years. Clay vessels were used for cooking, storing, and carrying food and water, as well as for ceremonial and burial purposes. Unlike many ancient cultures, the North American Indians didn't make wheel-thrown pottery. They hand-built their pots using older methods, such as coiling and modeling, and molded the bases inside a broken pot or over another container. Then, they baked the pots in an open fire to give the clay a stonelike finish.

Over time, different styles of pottery developed in different regions. The Wampanoag tribe, which celebrated Thanksgiving with the Pilgrims, made smooth coiled pottery decorated with incised lines around the rim. The finest North American Indian pottery is produced in the southwestern United States by the Pueblo Indians, who still use the coiling technique. The potters, traditionally women, developed a remarkable variety of geometric and abstract designs based on animal, plant, and insect motifs. Each *pueblo* (village) developed the distinctive shapes and decorative designs for which they are known today. The finest ancient and contemporary pieces are highly regarded as objects of fine art. Master Pueblo potters are world-renowned.

Materials

For each student:

- 2 to 2 1/2 lbs self-hardening clay (see Tip, page 41)
- 6 1/2- to 7-inch heavy paper plate with rim
- 2-inch pieces of sponge and Styrofoam
- shallow water container
- plastic knife
- plastic bag and twisters
- paper towels
- pencil
- scrap or graph paper
- Styrofoam tray (palette)

To share:

- black, white, red, and yellow paint
- paint brushes
- wooden stylus, toothpicks
- shells, rope, netting, and other objects for texture

For teacher:

- 1-foot fishing line
- two metal washers or pencils

About This Project

Creating a great piece of pottery requires experience, talent, and skill, but making a simple coiled pot is easy and fun. Even if students' pots turn out a little lopsided, they will enjoy learning this traditional pottery-making technique and exploring the inventive designs of this important Native American craft.

Students will build their pots with ropelike coils of clay that overlap slightly and spiral upward. They can smooth the walls and decorate their pots with impressed or incised designs, paint them with traditional decorative motifs, or leave the coils untouched for a corrugated effect. The pots won't need to be fired if you use a self-hardening (air-drying) clay.

Before You Begin

Show pictures of different types of Indian pottery. Cover desks with newspaper and distribute materials. Remind students to keep all unused clay in a plastic bag to prevent it from drying out.

Make the Clay Pot

1. Tell students that they'll use the paper plates to support the pot and turn it. To make the base, have students slice or break off a chunk of clay and roll it into a ball (about the size of a golf or tennis ball). Have them flatten the ball into a pancake (about 3/16-inch thick) with the heel of the hand. The base should be between 2 1/2 to 5 inches in diameter.

2. To make a coil, have students break off a piece of the remaining clay and roll it between their palms or on the desk with the heel of their hands. Tell them not to use their fingers or squeeze the clay. Use a gentle, even motion to make the coil the same thickness throughout—a little thicker than a pencil. Twelve inches is a good average length.

3. Have students cut the end of the coil at an angle with a plastic knife and score the end with a fingernail or toothpick. This will help make a better join when attaching coils.

4. Show students how to lay the first coil around the base, overlapping the end on top of itself slightly. Pinch the joints of the coil and base together inside and outside, then blend them together with an index finger in an up-and-down motion. Make sure there are no gaps between the joints.

5. Make two more coils and have students attach them the same way. If necessary moisten the clay with a damp sponge to help the coils stick together. Have them pinch the coils together along the joints and continue. Always attach a coil completely before rolling the next one.

● To make the pot grow wider, students should make a slightly longer coil, attach it along the outer edge of the wall, and make a wider spiral. (If the students find rolling a longer coil difficult, or if a coil breaks, they simply can attach two pieces together, as above.)

● To make the pot curve in, have students make a slightly tighter spiral (overlap the coil more) and attach it to the inner edge of the wall. Students can create a low open bowl or a jar with shoulders, neck, and rim by gradually expanding or tightening the coils in this way. Remind them to turn the plate as they work and moisten their hands or the coils if the clay starts to dry.

Tip

There are several brands of self-hardening (air-drying) clay. You may want to try a few samples before ordering for your class. Amaco makes two excellent brands: Mexican Pottery Clay, (terra-cotta) and Marblex (gray). For a large class, buy clay in 25-lb blocks. Slice through it with a tool made by tying a piece of fishing line between two metal washers or pencils.

Note

If students want to keep the corrugated surface on the outside of the bowl, they should pinch and blend the coils inside the pot only.

6. After every three layers of coils, have students smooth the inside walls with their index fingers or a piece of Styrofoam (moisten if necessary). They should cradle the pot on the outside with their other hand to support the pot and help keep its shape. Add a few more layers, blend, and continue. When they're finished building the pot, have students smooth the walls inside and outside. They can refine the shape while blending the coils together.

7. Have students scratch their initials on the bottom of their pots. If the pots aren't finished in one session, store them in tightly sealed plastic bags to keep the clay soft and pliable.

Decorate the Pot

1. Before students decorate their pots, have them make a few quick sketches of their pot (outline the shape) with some ideas for decorative designs. Working on graph paper will be helpful with geometric designs.

2. Students can decorate their pots by
   - **Impressing:** Press shells, netting, rope, the back of a stylus, or other objects into soft, damp clay. Roll objects evenly from left to right. Let students experiment first on a flat piece of clay.

   - **Incising:** Use a sharp pencil, toothpick, or wooden stylus to incise linear designs or scrape out shapes on the semidry or leather-hard surface (still damp but not malleable). To get the pots to this leather-hard stage, uncover students' pots the day before incising. When the pots are almost dry, wrap each one tightly in plastic to prevent it from drying out completely.

   - **Painting:** This should be done on pots that are completely dry (at least 48 hours in the open air). Students can apply a background color (white, tan, cream, or terra-cotta) with a wide foam or bristle brush over the exterior surface, or paint the designs directly on the clay. If they're applying a base coat, let it dry thoroughly before the next step. Paint the inside of the pot the same or a different color. Have them draw the designs only on the outside of the pot, unless they're decorating a wide, shallow bowl. They can paint the designs with black, white, or earth colors, or fill them in with fine black lines using a detail brush.

Tip

Cracks and breaks can be filled with plumber's epoxy after the pot is dry.

Note

Air-dried pottery isn't waterproof. You may want to coat or spray the pots with a matte acrylic varnish to seal and protect them. Even then, don't wash the pots or use them for food.

December

Theme: *Holiday Gifts*

December is a month for giving, and there's no better gift than one made by hand for someone you love. These projects will make wonderful gifts for family and friends.

Project 1: **Symbol Calendar**

Create a wall calendar decorated with symbols representing each month.

Sessions: 3–4

Curriculum Connection: Social Studies

Technique: Collage

Art Objectives: Graphic design, symbolism

Visual Vocabulary: Symbol, icon, logo, pictograph, collage

Art References: Graphic design and illustrations (icons, posters, brochures, album covers, greeting cards, etc.); Matisse collages; appliqué designs

Art Talk

Image-making is our first and oldest system of communication. Prehistoric cave paintings, petroglyphic drawings scratched into stone, carved picture seals—these images predate writing as symbols of communication. Images also formed the basis of several ancient-writing systems. Egyptian hieroglyphics used pictures to represent sounds. Chinese calligraphy is based on pictographic symbols that represent words or ideas. Medieval cathedrals were designed with the illiterate in mind. People "read" the Bible by studying the sculptures on the exterior of the building and the stained glass images inside.

Although we now have more advanced communication systems, we're still connected to symbolic visual language. Imagine a highway system without traffic or rest-stop symbols, a sneaker without a logo, or a computer without the user-friendly icons we've come to know so well. These images are shortcuts to communication. They're simple, universal symbols that everyone can understand. Graphic designers and illustrators use bold stylized images to get their messages across quickly and concisely. The Symbol Calendar will give your students an opportunity to explore the nature of symbolism and express their ideas in a visual way.

Materials

For each student:

- 6 copies of the Month Template (page 46)
- 12 or more 3-inch squares of drawing paper
- tracing paper
- 3-inch squares of colored construction paper (various colors)
- pencil
- scissors
- 2 plastic sandwich bags
- 12-inch cardboard square (posterboard or pizza box)
- newspaper

To share:

- glue sticks

For teacher:

- long-reach stapler
- calendar with dates
- mounting spray (optional)

About This Project

Symbolism is an abstract concept but one that students can easily grasp. Ask any child, "What image symbolizes the sport of ice skating?" or "What's a symbol for Halloween?" Once students get the concept, their ideas will flow. Then it's a matter of translating their ideas into simple and easily recognizable images.

Students will use cut-paper collage technique to create a simple colorful symbol for each month on a 3-inch square of colored construction paper. Together, these squares will form the decorative border of a 12-inch cardboard square. Students will add reproducible calendar pages, fill in months and dates, staple the pages together, and attach them to the center of the board.

Before You Begin

Discuss symbolism with your students. Explain that a symbol is something that represents another thing; for example, a flag symbolizes a country or a logo may symbolize a company. A symbol delivers a message without words, so it has to be a strong, simple image that everyone can understand quickly. Students will be making picture symbols to represent each month. They can use general symbols, sports symbols, or holiday symbols (e.g., a snowman for January, a football for September, a Christmas tree for December). Explain that colors also can be used as symbols (e.g., a red heart in February, a green shamrock in March). Have students brainstorm a list of ideas and bring in pictures of things they want to use as symbols.

Create the Symbol Designs and Make the Collages

1. Invite students to draw symbol ideas for each month on the drawing-paper squares. Have them draw simple outline shapes that fill the entire square. Tell them they will later cut up their drawings to make templates for the collages, so they don't have to include too many tiny details.

2. Have each student choose the best drawing for each month, then select colors for the cutouts and backgrounds. Help them choose contrasting colors for the cutouts so the designs stand out. Store the squares in plastic bags.

3. Students should work on one symbol at a time and keep the rest of the squares in the bag. Have them cut the template and colored paper together to make the cutout shapes. Instruct them to cut the biggest shape first, then reuse the template to cut the details in other colors. Save all scraps for cutting small details. Students can
- use tracing paper to make additional templates for overlapping shapes or details that conform to a shape. Place the tracing paper over the shape and outline the shape. Draw the details in outline form inside the shape on the tracing paper, then choose a color and cut the detail and template together.

- tear or cut other details without a template. Eyes, buttons, or snow can be made with a hole punch.

4. Have students glue each collage onto its background square before moving on to the next one. Store finished collages in another plastic bag.

5. When students have finished making all their collages, have them glue the collages to the 12-inch cardboard. Begin with January in the top left corner and continue clockwise around the cardboard. Remind them to make sure the pieces fit snugly without overlapping each other or the edges of the board.

Complete the Calendar

1. Have students cut out the Month Templates and staple them together.

2. Invite them to fill in the dates and months (write the names on the board for proper spelling) with a marker. Or write the starting and ending dates for each month and have students fill in the rest at home. Encourage them to add holidays and special events.

3. Glue or staple the last month of the calendar to the center of the cardboard.

Tip

Add a strip of magnetic tape to the back of the board so kids can hang the calendar on a refrigerator.

Month Template

SUNDAY	MONDAY	TUESDAY	WEDNESDAY	THURSDAY	FRIDAY	SATURDAY

SUNDAY	MONDAY	TUESDAY	WEDNESDAY	THURSDAY	FRIDAY	SATURDAY

December

Project 2: **Gift Box**

Design a cardboard-box construction filled with symbolic objects.

Sessions: 2–3

Curriculum Connection: Social Studies

Technique: Mixed-media assemblage

Art Objective: 3-dimensional design

Visual Vocabulary: Box construction, assemblage, collage, found objects, texture, symmetrical, asymmetrical, columns, pedestals, architecture, symbolism

Art References: Victorian shadow boxes; **Box Constructions:** Joseph Cornell, Marcel Duchamp, Lucas Samaras, and Louise Nevelson

Art Talk

The box constructions of American artist Joseph Cornell are the inspiration for this project. A shy, reclusive man, Cornell created a private world of lyrical beauty in the small boxes he found or made himself. These constructions are a three-dimensional form of collage (or assemblage)—skillful arrangements of colors, shapes, and textures made with found or inexpensive objects and materials.

Cornell's works have a surreal dreamlike quality, achieved with symbolic juxtaposition of images and objects. Many are nostalgic reminders of childhood—boxes filled with shifting sands, penny arcades, or shadow-box theaters with dancing paper puppets. These all have elements that move and make sounds when they're tilted or cranked. Cornell scoured beaches, dime stores, and bookshops in search of materials—driftwood, seeds, twigs, watch springs, dolls, old illustrations, photographs, sheet music, and newspaper clippings. He painted or lined his boxes with velvet, mirrors, and natural materials. Columns or geometric grids suggest classical or modern architecture. Cornell filled cubbies, bottles, and drawers with colored glass, crushed minerals, and bits of string. Cornell's boxes were often made as homages (tributes) or gifts for people he admired. Each is an intimate world—intellectually sophisticated, yet filled with childlike wonder. Children, in fact, were his favorite audience. He believed they understood his work best.

Materials

For each student:

- corrugated cardboard box with flaps (about 4- to 6-inches deep, 10- to 14-inches high, 9- to 12-inches wide)
- found objects and collage materials (see page 49)
- pencil
- scissors
- toilet paper or paper towel tubes (optional)
- smaller boxes (optional)

To share:

- paint
- white glue
- rulers or T-squares
- string or fishing line
- assorted objects, such as shells, feathers, buttons (optional)
- pointy compass

For teacher:

- glue gun (optional)

About This Project

Like Cornell and other assemblage artists, students will begin their project with a treasure hunt. They'll collect objects that symbolically represent themselves or the gift recipient. Then they'll arrange the objects inside a cardboard box, which they'll divide into sections and paint or cover with decorative materials.

This project will make students more aware of the colors, shapes, and textures of everyday objects. They'll also begin to understand how artists use assemblage to transform ordinary things into a work of art. This project can also be a lesson about architectural and three-dimensional design as students figure out ways to partition their boxes and break up space in exciting ways.

Before You Begin

Show your students pictures of box constructions (or other types of assemblage). Ask them to find and bring in objects and materials that symbolize things they (or the gift recipient) like to collect, wear, or enjoy doing. They shouldn't buy anything or bring in anything valuable. Remind students to choose things with interesting textures and colors, in different shapes and sizes, that will look good together.

They should also bring in a box. If possible, have them prepare the box at home: Cut off the top flaps as neatly as possible. The box should be as deep as the width of the flaps. If the box is too deep, cut down the sides. Peel off unwanted labels and excess tape to provide a good surface for paint.

Plan the Design

1. Invite students to sort through their objects and decide how they should be arranged in the box. The emphasis should be on design—how things relate in terms of color, size, texture, and shape. Encourage children to trade objects with friends or eliminate objects that would create too much clutter.

2. Have students decide on a horizontal or vertical format and think of interesting ways to divide the interior space based on the size and shape of their objects. They can hang objects or divide the space using the flaps, cardboard cylinders, or smaller boxes.

Divide the Space

1. There are two ways students can use the flaps as dividers:

   ● They can start with the longest flap and glue it in place. Then they can measure, cut, and glue the shorter flaps to the first flap and the box. Wherever possible, brace the dividers against the remaining (closed) flaps inside the back of the box for added support. You can use a glue gun or students can use white glue. Working in pairs, one student should hold the divider in place while the other presses the box against it until the glue dries.

   ● To make a sturdier joint, students can intersect the dividers. Show them how to cut a slot (about the same thickness as the cardboard) halfway across each flap, then slip the flaps into each other. Adjust the fit, then glue.

2. Students can use cardboard tubes to make columns and support shelves. Pedestals, shelves, or drawers can be made with small boxes. They can also create divisions by hanging objects with string, heavy thread, or yarn. Remind students not to knot or glue the hanging objects in place until the box is painted or covered with collage material.

3. Students can cover a section in front of the box with cardboard and glue textured materials or objects to the surface. Cutting a shape in the cardboard will make it more interesting. The cut-out shape can become a peephole by placing an object behind it. Mesh, lace, colored or paint-splattered plastic, or twigs can be used as semitransparent screens.

Assemble Objects and Paint the Box

1. When students have finished the interior construction, have them assemble their objects to see how they look inside the box. Have them choose background colors and textures. They can use one color or different colors for each section and add wallpaper, fabric, and other collage materials. Everything should work well together to create a unified design. Tell students not to glue down anything yet.

2. Have students remove the objects and paint the entire box (except the outer bottom) with a few coats of tempera paint.

3. Have students glue the objects in place with white glue (or you can do it for them with a glue gun). For hanging objects, poke a hole through the box and pull the string through the hole, knot it, and glue the knot to the top of the box or partition.

Gift Box Ideas

Yo-yo, ball, toy cars, blocks, jacks, marbles, boats, planes, Lego pieces, gameboard pieces, crayons, film, coins, old CDs, buttons, baby shoes, nail polish, ribbon, barrettes, costume jewelry, string, yarn, thread spools, keys, compass, candy, pasta, soda can, rocks, feathers, shells, starfish, pressed flowers, leaves, twigs, pine cones, stamps, stickers, map, sheet music, comics, magazine pictures of singers or movie stars, postcards, sports cards, family snapshots, fabric, wallpaper, lace

January

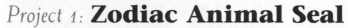

Theme: New Year Celebrations
Everyone rejoices at the beginning of a New Year. Chinese New Year celebrations are filled with many symbolic ancient traditions. We've adapted two for these projects.

Project 1: **Zodiac Animal Seal**
Create a personal seal topped with a sculpture of a Chinese zodiac animal.

Session: 1
Curriculum Connection: Social Studies
Technique: Sculpture
Art Objectives: Figurative sculpture, monograms
Visual Vocabulary: Seal, chop, calligraphy, monogram
Art References: Zodiac animals used in Chinese folk and decorative art

Art Talk

The Chinese New Year (also called the Spring Festival) begins on the first day of the new moon on the Chinese lunar calendar (between January 21 and February 20 on the Western calendar). Each year is represented by one of the twelve Chinese zodiac animals. Unlike the 12-month cycle of the Western zodiac, the animal zodiac is a 12-year cycle that begins with the Year of the Rat (see page 51). Each animal has distinctive traits, which are said to determine the character and fate of people born under its sign. The animal zodiac is part of a more complex zodiac system (based on a 60-year cycle) that played an important role in Chinese culture for more than 2,000 years.

Carved seals also were used in China for more than 2,000 years. Today, they're still used as signatures on documents and paintings. Made from a variety of stones, they're carved in an old calligraphic style known as "seal script" and printed with a waxy red ink. Anyone can buy a blank seal (also called a chop) and have it carved with their initials. They come in different sizes and are usually cylindrical or rectangular in shape. Often, they're topped with small sculptures, like the zodiac animals the students will create for this project.

About This Project

Students love modeling in clay and they will enjoy this quick, easy, and imaginative project. They will sculpt a clay zodiac animal representing the year of their birth or the current year. They'll attach the sculpture to a clay base and carve their initials on the bottom. They can use their personal seals to stamp cards, stationery, or even their homework!

Before You Begin

Have students bring in pictures (or toy models) of animals for reference. Divide the clay for each child and keep any extra clay tightly sealed in its container. Have students cover their desks with newspaper. Distribute the clay materials: clay, water tins, sponges, plastic knives or rulers, toothpicks, plastic wrap or sandwich bags. (Save the materials for their stamps until they're ready for that step.)

Make the Base and Sculpture

1. Have students decide on a shape for the pedestal base (cube, rectangle, or cylinder) and think about how they want to represent their animal. Remind them that long skinny legs may not support a standing figure. They can sculpt the animal in a seated pose or just sculpt the head. A head will fit on a narrow base, while a standing or seated animal will need a wider base. Students can also have parts of the animal overlap the base. For example, a dragon's tail or a snake could wrap around the base.

2. Have students divide their clay in half. Use one part for the base. Save the rest for the sculpture and seal it in plastic.

Materials

For each student:

- 1/2 lb self-hardening clay (see Tip, page 41)
- newspaper
- plastic sandwich bags
- pencil and marker
- scrap and tracing paper
- small pieces of Styrofoam

To share:

- toothpicks, wooden stylus
- plastic knives or ruler
- small pieces of sponge
- shallow cans for water
- stamp pads (or a sponge and tempera paint)
- scissors (optional)
- white glue (optional)

For teacher:

- plastic wrap or bags
- 1 1/2-foot wire or fishing line (for dividing clay blocks)
- 2 pencils or metal washers
- clear acrylic spray varnish (optional)

3. Show students how to roll the clay on the table to make a cylinder about 2- to 2 1/2-inches high by 3/4- to 1 1/2-inches wide. If they want to make a rectangular shape, they can flatten the sides by tamping the clay on the table. They also can roll the clay into a ball and turn it into a cube. (Remind students not to squeeze the clay or their finger impressions will remain when it hardens. If they do, have them smooth the surface with the sponge or add pieces of clay and blend it in.)

4. Show students how to trim the top and bottom of their bases with a plastic knife or ruler, or tamp the ends gently on the desk to smooth and flatten them. If necessary wipe the surface with the sponge. The base has to be perfectly smooth and flat to print well. Have students seal their bases in plastic while they make the sculpture.

5. Before students begin to sculpt, have them knead the clay to make it more supple. Remind them that a sculpture is a three-dimensional object that should look good from every angle. They should turn their sculpture as they work.

6. Encourage students to add texture to their figures (e.g., fur, scales, feathers). They can use a pointy implement, such as a toothpick, or add on bits of clay.

7. To attach the animal to the base, students should first roughen the surfaces of the sculpture and base that will be joined together. They should scrape shallow lines across the surfaces with their fingernails or a toothpick and moisten the clay before attaching them. Pinch and blend the clay together until the seams disappear. Students can use the Styrofoam piece for blending and smoothing. Have them double-check the bottom of their bases to make sure they're flat and smooth.

Add Initials and Stamp the Seals

1. Students can engrave their initials on the bottom of the base with a pencil or wooden stylus. It's best to do this when the clay is leather hard, which will take a few hours. If the clay isn't ready by the end of the day, cover the seals loosely with plastic to prevent them from drying out completely and engrave them the next day.

2. IMPORTANT: Remind students that seals print in reverse, so they will have to write their initials backward. First, have them trace around the bottom of the base on tracing paper. Then have them write their initials (the usual way) within the shape they traced. If there's enough room, they can write their entire name, draw a border around the letters, or create an interesting monogram or logo design. When they're done, have students turn over the tracing paper and copy the reversed image on the base.

3. Let the seals dry completely before printing. Self-hardening clay isn't waterproof; a coat or two of acrylic spray varnish will help seal the clay. (Keep the window open and spray when the students are out of the room.) Even then, don't wash or wet the seals.

4. To print the seal, use a commercial stamp pad or make your own by putting some tempera paint on a damp sponge. (Use paint only with varnished clay or Styrofoam engraving.) The clay stamp will print better if the paper is cushioned. Put a piece of Styrofoam or some newspapers under the paper. Press the seal into the stamp pad, then press or rock it slightly on the paper to make the impression. (Remind students that unfired clay is fragile and should be handled with care.)

Tip

You also may want to have students engrave their initials into a piece of Styrofoam. If the clay doesn't print well (the surface may not be flat enough or may absorb the ink) students can glue the Styrofoam engraving to the base. They should place their tracing (reversed) over the Styrofoam and cut out the base shape. Copy the reversed initials on to the Styrofoam with a marker, then engrave with a pencil or stylus. Press hard to make a clear impression.

January

Project 2: Chinese Lion Dance Festival Mask

Create a papier-mâché lion dance mask to celebrate the New Year.

Sessions: 5–8

Curriculum Connections: Social Studies, Literature

Art Objectives: Sculpture, anatomy, painting

Visual Vocabulary: Papier-mâché, armature, symmetry, stylized, realistic, decorative, symbolic

Art References: Chinese and other festival masks; ritual masks (African, Oceanic, Northwest Coast); death masks (Pre-Colombian and Egyptian mummy masks); ancient war masks; high-tech masks; drama, carnival, and Halloween masks

Art Talk

Mask-making is one of the world's oldest and most inventive cultural traditions. Masks are made in every conceivable shape, style, and material, and serve all sorts of functions. They can be magical ritual objects; fanciful or practical objects; and outstanding works of sculpture made with great imagination and skill.

Chinese festival masks are highly stylized folk-art creations. The lion masks are made of papier-mâché, a technique originated in China, where paper making was invented. They're an integral part of the ancient lion-dance tradition, which originally served a ritual function and later became a symbolic enactment of ancient lion myths and folk tales. Two dancers assume the lion role—one wears the mask and manipulates the moveable eyes, ears, and mouth like a puppeteer, while the other controls the cloth body. They mimic the lion's comic habits and perform acrobatic feats, while the rest of the colorful troupe set off firecrackers and beat cymbals, drums, and gongs to scare away evil spirits and assure good luck and prosperity.

The masks are made in different styles. North American lion masks are extravagantly decorated with pom-poms, fiber, and flamboyant designs painted over a solid background color that symbolizes the lion's personality and role. Black lions are young, aggressive, and mischievous; white-bearded lions are the sages; headstrong red lions represent the god of war; and their aides, the gold or yellow lions, symbolize prosperity.

About This Project

Making this large over-the-head papier-mâché mask is time consuming but very easy. Just set up the basic structure (cardboard and Styrofoam features taped to a stuffed paper bag), then build and refine the forms with successive layers of newspaper strips dipped in a mixture of white glue and water. The final step is painting the mask with decorative designs. Students will learn about anatomy, sculpture, painting, and decorative design, and they'll love having a mask to wear and display. You can use this technique for other holidays—Halloween, Carnival, or Purim—or to sculpt other types of objects.

Before You Begin

Discuss masks and their functions with students and show examples. Have each students tear (not cut) the newspaper strips at home. (Torn edges blend better.) A loosely filled grocery bag should be enough to finish each mask. Use plain newsprint or kraft paper for the last layer. (It's a better surface for drawing and painting designs.)

Use cardboard drink-carrying trays for the triangular nose forms. One tray will make four noses. Cut the tray apart, discard the center, and trim around the forms. Start a sample mask. Attach the forms for the features and cover half the mask with a layer of papier-mâché. Cover the other half in class to demonstrate the technique. Discuss symmetry and the basic shape and placement of facial features. Ask a parent to assist with the first two sessions.

Make the Armature (1 session)

The armature is the framework of a sculpture. For this mask, the armature is a stuffed paper bag. Students will add cardboard and Styrofoam forms to establish the features before beginning the papier-mâché.

1. Assign students to work in pairs to shape the bags:
    - Have one student pull the bag over her head, while the partner turns up the bottom edge to make a cuff (about 3 inches) at the base of her neck. The first student should gently squeeze the bag around her own neck to shape the bag.

Materials

For each student:

- Head: medium-size brown paper bag
- Ears: Styrofoam cups
- Nose: one section of a cardboard drink-carrying tray (from fast-food restaurant)
- Mouth: 7-inch stiff paper plate
- Teeth: Styrofoam (optional)
- toilet-paper tube
- scissors
- 11- by 16 1/2-inch disposable aluminum tray
- bag of torn newspaper strips (about 1 1/2 inches wide)
- pencil
- copy paper
- Styrofoam tray (palette)
- kraft (brown wrapping) paper or plain white newsprint strips (optional)
- 2-inch utility bristle brush (optional)

(continued on next page)

Materials
(continued)

To share:

- marker or crayon
- masking tape
- paper towels (a roll for each session)
- plastic bowls
- newspaper
- tempera paint
- small detail brushes
- 1-inch and 1 1/2-inch foam or bristle brushes
- containers for paint and water
- mixing sticks

For teacher:

- measuring cup
- buckets for water
- mixing sticks
- white glue (3–4 gallons for a class of 25)
- Kraft or Exacto knife
- glue gun (optional)
- clear acrylic spray varnish (optional)

- To create flaps that rest on the student's shoulders, have the partner make 2-inch tears at the four corners of the cuff. (Remind students to be careful because tearing too much will rip the neck and it will loose its shape.)

- Have the partner gently press down the corners on top of the bag to conform to the shape of the first student's head and tape them down.

- Have the first student point a finger to the center of her eyes. Using a marker or a crayon, the partner should draw circles around the fingers to indicate eye placement. **IMPORTANT:** Do not use a pointy object like a pencil or pen.

- Finally, have the student remove the paper bag. The neck will spread a little to allow the child's head to emerge. The neck becomes the size of the head opening.

2. Tell partners to switch roles and repeat the first step. After they have shaped their bags, have students stuff them firmly with balls of crumpled newspaper. Remind them to be careful not to distort the shape.

3. Have students write their names with a marker on a piece of masking tape and attach it underneath the tray. Have them tape the flaps of their bags to an aluminum tray.

4. Have students make the features and attach them to the bag with masking tape (or you can do it with a glue gun):
   - Center the nose (piece of cardboard tray) just below the eye markings.

   - For each eye, twist two strips of newspaper together, fold in half, then twist again. Form the twisted paper into a circle, tape it together, and attach it around the eye-hole markings to form a ridged outline.

- Make the mouth: Fold the paper plate in half. Hold the folded edge between the teeth and pull the plate around the cheeks to shape it. Pull a long strip of masking tape across the fold (or use hot glue) and attach it to the bag.

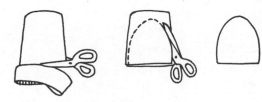

● For each ear, cut off the bottom of a Styrofoam cup. Flatten the cup by pressing the sides together. (It's okay if the cup cracks.) Hold the sides together as you do these next steps: Cut off the rim. Trim the edge neatly. Cut around the rest of the cup to form the shape of a lion's ear. Attach the ears after the first layer of papier-mâché is finished.

Cover with Papier-mâché and Refine Features (3-5 sessions)

Papier-mâché is built up in layers. To keep track of the layers and make a better bond, alternate vertical and horizontal strips. Use as many layers as necessary to make the mask rigid (three layers should be sufficient).

1. Divide students into groups so they can share materials for the remaining steps. Cover the desks and floor with a few layers of newspaper.

2. Mix two parts glue to one part warm water in a large bucket to make a gallon of glue mixture. The mixture should have a light consistency that's tacky to the touch. Distribute the glue in wide plastic bowls. (Save any excess solution for the next session.)

3. Demonstrate how to apply the strips to the papier-mâché:
● Dip one end of a newspaper strip in the bowl and drag the strip through the solution. Slide the strip between two fingers to squeeze off the excess glue. (Too much glue will make the form soggy, and the strips won't hold well. It also will take too long to dry between layers.)

● Try to place all the strips in one direction. Slightly overlap the strips. When necessary, tear them into smaller pieces to bend around the features, such as the ridged circle around the eyes.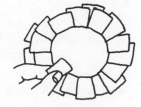

● Press the strips firmly around the forms. If the paper is not pressed down tightly, gaps will form between the layers and create unwanted edges that will harden when dry. They can be filled in later with wadded newspaper or paper towels dipped in the solution, but it's best to try to avoid that step.

Tip

Students can brush the glue-and-water solution on the mask after the first layer dries instead of dipping the strips. Coat one section at a time, add the dry strips, then coat the next section, and continue. Coat everything with glue before the end of the session. As the masks dry between sessions, they'll become more rigid and easier to work on.

4. Have students papier-mâché one layer, including the neck and flaps. The neck and flaps will help support the mask after the first layer dries and can be cut off after the mask is finished. Keep the mouth in a half-opened position (the top lip should be in a relatively flat or horizontal position) and cover the plate completely (inside and out) with papier-mâché. (If the paper plate gets soggy and starts to close, prop it open with a toilet-paper tube.)

5. Before beginning the second layer, have students attach the ears. If the mask is dry, you can quickly attach the ears with a few dots of hot glue, or students can tack them on with masking tape. They also can use long strips of papier-mâché that go over the ears from front to back. Anchor them with perpendicular strips at the junction.

6. When the mask is rigid enough (after the first or second layer), have the students put it on to check the eye position. If the eyes are in the right position, have the students take off the bag and poke holes through the eyes with a pencil and widen the opening a bit with their finger. (Don't make the holes too big.) Bind the edges with little pieces of papier-mâché. Continue building the raised outline around the eyes in successive layers with little pieces of papier-mâché.

NOTE: If the eyes aren't in the right place, remove the ridged outlines with a kraft knife (be careful not to cut the bag). Then relocate the eyes. Cover up the mistake with new layers of papier-mâché. Any part can be removed and repaired this way, if necessary.

7. Students can add or enhance facial features (e.g., eyebrows, cheeks, nostrils) using crumpled or twisted coils of newspaper or paper towel dipped in the solution. Simply press the formed paper onto the surface and cover them with gluey strips of newspaper.

8. Use plain white newsprint or kraft paper to make strips for the last layer. Let the mask dry thoroughly before painting.

Paint and Decorate the Mask (1-2 sessions)

Read and discuss Painting (page 9). Painting the mask will pull everything together. A clever use of color can help hide sculptural mistakes or create features that haven't been sculpted, such as eyebrows and nostrils.

1. Have students make some quick sketches on scrap or copy paper outlining the shape and features of their mask. Have students sketch some decorative designs with pencil or colored markers (e.g., flames, wavy or jagged lines, curlicues, dots).

2. Have students draw their designs on the mask with a pencil and select a background color.

3. Prepare bowls of paint. Distribute water tins, paper towels, palettes, large brushes for background colors, and smaller brushes for details.

4. Remind students to use contrasting colors to make the features and designs stand out. There are several ways students can paint their masks:

- Use a detail brush to paint the outlines with the background color, and paint the rest of the background with a broader brush. To produce hard, sharp edges, wait for the paint to dry before painting in the designs and features.

- Cover the entire mask with the background color. When the background paint dries, paint the features and details. This works best with light-colored backgrounds.

- Paint background and design together to blend colors and create soft edges.

To protect and seal the paint, you can brush or spray on a clear acrylic varnish in a well-ventilated room.

5. Students can add more details to their masks: teeth (paint them or cut them out of Styrofoam and glue them on), pom-poms, a fringed beard (cut or curled paper, felt, raffia, fake fur, or upholstery fringe), whiskers (broom bristles), or glitter. They can also attach a cloth costume to the neck by gluing Velcro strips along the edges, or poking holes in the flaps and sewing on the fabric with thread.

Celebrate!

Celebrate the completion of the masks with an ancient tradition still practiced today: Before a new costume is worn, the lion must be brought to life in a ritual ceremony that awakens his senses. Dot the eyes, ears, and tongue with red paint to allow the lion to see, hear, and taste. A dot on the head and spine gives it the ability to think and move. An awakening ceremony would help the students understand the ritual functions of a mask. It's a great way to conclude the project and begin the New Year.

February

Theme: **Great American Themes**

The month we celebrate our presidents is a good time to learn about design with a historical slant—flags and early American quilt design.

Project 1: **Flag Design**

Design a flag that symbolizes your class or school.

Sessions: 2–3

Curriculum Connections: Social Studies, Math

Technique: Collage

Art Objective: Symbolic design

Visual Vocabulary: Symbol, emblem, logo, heraldic design, canton (or union), field, proportion, scale

Art References: National, organizational (team, school, military, etc.), and signal flags

Art Talk

Flags are symbols that have been used to identify groups of people for thousands of years. While flags today are made of cloth, their forerunners were made of all kinds of materials, such as solid disks mounted on poles or fans of exotic feathers. Early cloth flags were plain, or displayed simple picture symbols on a solid background.

During medieval times, flag design became more complex. The flags of kings, knights, and noblemen displayed the heraldic symbols of their crests—stylized plants, animals, mythical beasts, castles, and geometric motifs. The field (or background) often was divided into specific sections with bars, chevrons, or other devices. All elements were arranged according to specific rules of heraldic design, which influenced flag design for centuries. Early national European flags were more simplified. Many featured crosses (for the country's patron saint) on a solid background. Some modern flags still display religious symbols or contain elements of heraldic design. A few use bold picture symbols, while many others are dynamic abstract arrangements of simple shapes and symbolic colors.

By studying early designs of the American flag (page 61), your class will learn an important lesson about design. The slightest variation in the proportion, direction, color, size, or shape of any element will create an entirely new design. If you look at a chart of national flags, you'll see that three of the most widely used devices—stripes or bars, crosses, and stars and crescents—appear in more than 100 flags, yet each flag is unique.

Designing the American Flag

According to legend, George Washington left the heat of battle to bring a sketch of the Stars and Stripes (which resembled his family crest) to a Philadelphia seamstress named Betsy Ross. She changed the six-pointed star to five and sewed the first flag of the fledgling nation. Although it's a great story, there's no evidence that the Stars and Stripes existed during the Revolution. Others laid claim to the honor, but no one really knows who designed the American flag. What we do know is that its appearance kept changing.

In 1777, the first flag law simply designated 13 alternating red-and-white stripes and 13 white stars representing a "new constellation" set on a blue union. (Americans call the canton, the upper quarter section nearest the staff, a union.) But the law didn't specify the proportion or position of any of these elements. The results were chaotic. Some flags had vertical stripes; others had horizontal stripes. Some flags had seven white and six red stripes; others had six white and seven red stripes. The size of the union varied, and the stars were laid out in circles, semicircles, or rows. Things got more confusing as more states were created. The famous Star Spangled Banner (1814) had 15 stars and stripes! Finally, in 1912, a law was passed that specified every detail.

Materials

For each student:

- 1/4-inch and 1-inch graph paper
- pencil and eraser
- ruler
- 9- by 12-inch colored construction paper or felt (wool/rayon blend) in assorted colors
- scissors
- wooden dowel (3/16- by 12-inches)

To share:

- colored markers, crayons, or pencils
- compass
- hole punch
- glue sticks (for paper)
- white or tacky glue (for felt)

About This Project

This project will give students an opportunity to explore concepts of symbolism and basic design. They also will develop math and measurement skills as they learn about scale and proportion and how to use graph paper. Each student will design a class flag using pictorial, geometric, or linear elements as symbols. The finished flag will be a collage made out of colored construction paper or felt.

Before You Begin

Discuss the American flag, flag design, and symbolism. Show and compare different types of flags. Explain that a flag can be a symbol by itself (a unique arrangement of colors and shapes) or can be composed of symbolic elements. Invite students to make a list of things that symbolize their class or school (e.g., the total number of students, the numbers of boys and girls, notebooks, or the school mascot). Explain how they can use these elements as class symbols (25 balloons or dots can represent 25 kids; 15 blue and 10 red balloons can represent boys and girls). They can use the number just by itself (a big 25) or combine it with other graphic elements.

Point out the different ways symbols can be arranged. Students can spread the symbols across the field, divide the field into sections and place different symbols in each section, place them in the canton, or use one central symbol.

Design the Flag and Make Templates

1. Distribute the 1/4-inch graph paper. Tell students they will be creating formats for their thumbnail sketches that are scaled to the same proportions as the finished flag (10- by 6-inches).

2. Have students outline the formats. They can count graph boxes (10 boxes across and 6 down) or use a ruler to measure and draw them. To fit the maximum number of formats on the graph paper, students should place the first one near the top corner. Remind them to leave space between formats (at least one graph box) and make them all horizontal.

3. Have students make thumbnail sketches of different designs. Encourage them to draw outlines of simple shapes and figures. They can count graph boxes to help them create bars of equal width or height, find the center of the format, and so on. Have students use rulers and compasses to draw geometric shapes. Have them color each sketch with markers or crayons. Help them choose a bold and simple design that will work best as a flag.

4. Distribute the 1-inch graph paper. Have students draw a 10- by 6-inch format and enlarge their best sketch into a full-size outline drawing to use as a template. (To enlarge the sketch on 1-inch graph paper, have students enlarge the shapes by counting the same number of boxes as in the 1/4-inch graph paper.) They can make numbers or letters on a computer and use them as templates.

5. Have students cut the graph paper to make templates. Cut only one template for repetitive shapes (e.g., if they're making a checkerboard pattern, they'll need only one template to cut all the squares). For concentric shapes or shapes within shapes, cut only the outer (largest) shape. After students use the largest shape as a template, they can cut it down to the next size. Fold symmetrical shapes in half and trim the template to make both sides perfectly even.

Cut the Material and Make the Flag

1. Have students measure and cut the background material into a 6- by 10 1/2-inch format. (The extra 1/2 inch will wrap around the stick.) Lightly draw a vertical line 1/2-inch from the left edge with a pencil. Collect the scraps and save them for small shapes.

2. Students should use their templates to cut the shapes. For two-sided flags, cut the material in duplicate.

3. Tell students to arrange all the pieces on the background. Remind them not to go past the pencil line. Leave all the pieces in place.

4. Have students glue on one piece at a time, working from the top layer down. Put glue on the back of the combined shape and attach the whole thing to the next layer. If the students are making paper flags, have them use glue sticks. For felt flags, they should use white or tacky glue (just a few dots in the center of the shape and around the perimeter).

5. To attach sticks, have students measure six inches from the top of the dowel and mark it with a pencil. Place the dowel on a piece of newspaper. Squeeze beads of white glue from the top of the stick to the 6-inch mark. Place the stick glue-side down on the flag a bit away from the edge, leaving enough material to roll over the stick. Add more glue to the stick and roll the material around it. Press the material to the stick and hold it in place for a few minutes. Then, wave the flag!

Tip

Students who are making a one-sided flag should turn over the flag and glue the stick to the back. Make sure they glue it to the correct edge of the flag!

February

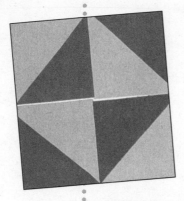

Project 2: Block-Style Quilt Design

Create a geometric quilt design with colored construction paper.

Sessions: 2–3

Curriculum Connections: Math, Social Studies

Technique: Collage

Art Objective: Geometric design

Visual Vocabulary: Block, pattern, geometric, motif, rotate, flop, diagonal

Art References: Block-style quilts; tile or mosaic geometric patterns

Art Talk

Quilt making didn't originate in the United States, but it flourished here between the late 18th and 19th centuries and became one of America's great folk art and design traditions. Like most folk art, quilts were made to serve a function—people needed warm blankets so women sandwiched a filler between two layers of cloth and stitched them together to make a quilt. The top layer could be made of plain whole cloth or decorated with appliqued designs. Since cloth was expensive women saved scraps of fabric—often from used clothes—and pieced them together in different ways to make the top cloth. The block-style piecing method was a distinctive American innovation. It's based on a geometrically designed square (the block) that's reproduced in multiples and usually linked together to form an overall design. Linking the blocks in different ways can produce a multitude of dazzling patterns.

Working in small, repetitive units was more efficient than the older method of progressive piecing, and the flexible geometric system gave rural women a practical approach to creative design. American women devised hundreds of sophisticated block designs with motifs based on anything that touched their lives. The great variety of themes are reflected in their block titles: Underground Railroad, Jacob's Ladder, Bear's Paw, Log Cabin, Broken Dishes, Shoo Fly. Women took great pride in exhibiting their quilts and competed for prizes in craftsmanship and design. Many of these folk-art works bear a striking resemblance to American abstract paintings, which they predated by at least a century!

About This Project

This project will give students a chance to explore the exciting world of geometric design. For this project, students will create the simplest block design—a four-patch block made of four squares that are each divided into two triangles. First, students will cut and glue a triangle in a contrasting color on each square. Then they'll arrange the squares into a block design. Once they have the design (the master block), they'll copy it to make five more blocks, arrange them into a linked-block pattern, and glue the pieces onto paper. Students will love making—and solving—this geometric puzzle.

Before You Begin

There are two ways to approach this project: If you're short on time or want perfect squares, cut the 3-inch squares yourself on a paper cutter. Cut a variety of colors (about two sheets per student) and sort the squares by color. Or, if you want students to practice their measuring and cutting skills, have them cut the squares themselves. Use rulers or T-squares (page 73).

To demonstrate how to make a design, cut two squares diagonally to make triangles. Glue the triangles onto four 3-inch squares. Create different block designs by moving the squares into different positions. Prepare at least four finished blocks of one design and show children how to create different patterns by linking them together in different ways. Create the Windmill design (see illustration) with extra triangles by partially overlapping the triangle in each square.

WINDMILL

NOTE: Demonstrate without having the kids do it along with you. You want them to get the idea, but have fun figuring out the "puzzle" (the designs) themselves.

Make Blocks and Create a Pattern

1. Have students select their squares (choose two contrasting colors, 24 squares of each color).

2. Have students cut one set of squares into triangles. They can draw a diagonal line across one square or use a cardboard template as a guide and cut a few squares at the same time. Keep all the edges aligned.

3. Show students how to glue a triangle on each square. (See Gluing, page 8.) Make sure the corners match up. Store triangles, plain and unfinished squares in separate plastic bags.

Materials

For each student:

- 3 sheets of 12- by 18-inch colored construction paper
- pencil
- scissors
- plastic sandwich bag
- ruler (optional)
- cardboard triangle template cut from a 3-inch square (optional)
- six 6-inch squares of drawing or colored construction paper (optional)

To share:

- glue sticks
- masking tape
- newspaper
- felt
- white or tacky glue (optional)

For teacher:

- samples for demonstration

Keep Going!

Create more exciting patterns by adding new triangles in a different color to the design. Partially overlap one of the original colors (Windmill design) or cut the new triangles in half or quarters to create more intricate designs (use the cardboard template as a guide). Experiment with a few designs, then arrange and glue new pieces on one block to create a master block. Copy it to complete the pattern.

Make a class quilt with felt. Pick one block design. Have each student make a block, arrange all the blocks into a pattern, then glue them to a felt backing with white or tacky glue.

4. Have students arrange four squares into different block designs. Start by facing all the lighter colored triangles the same way and rotate one piece at a time.

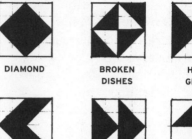
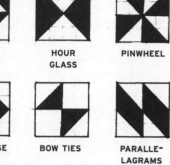

5. Once students have chosen a block design, they can tape the squares together to make the master block. Have them lay a 4-inch piece of masking tape, sticky side up, next to the block. Stick one square at a time to a section of the tape to temporarily hold the block together. (They'll remove the tape when they glue the squares to the drawing paper.) They can also glue the four squares to a 6-inch square of matching colored construction paper.

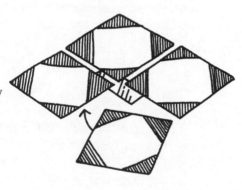

6. Using the master block for reference, have the students make five more blocks using the rest of the squares and tape them together (or glue them to 6-inch squares).

7. Give each child a 12- by 18-inch sheet of matching colored construction paper and let them create different linked patterns by rotating, flipping (turn upside down) or flopping (mirror image) their blocks.

8. When the students have decided on a pattern, they should leave all the blocks in place. If the blocks are taped together, have them gently pull the tape off one block at a time and glue each piece to the large construction paper. Have them repeat with the next block, and so on. Refer to the block design when gluing to keep up the pattern. Or, they can attach the glued-up 6-inch blocks one at a time. Remind students to make all the edges meet and avoid overlapping.

March

Theme: *Wind and Motion*

Air currents are a source of energy and motion. Windy March is the perfect time to explore this subject with two wind-related projects.

Project 1: **Abstract Mobile**

Learn about balance and design an abstract hanging mobile.

Sessions: 2–3

Curriculum Connection: Science

Techniques: Sculpture, painting

Art Objectives: Kinetic sculpture, abstract design

Visual Vocabulary: Open, closed, geometric, and freeform shapes, spiral, sphere, abstract design, kinetic, static, balance (visual & physical)

Art Reference: Alexander Calder

Art Talk

Alexander Calder invented the mobile, a form of sculpture that makes movement an important element of its design. While most sculpture is solid and static, Calder's mobiles are light, airy kinetic works made of wire and various materials.

Drawing upon his earlier training as a mechanical engineer, Calder's first mobiles were motor-driven or hand-cranked. But the mechanical movements were too regular and repetitious. His interest in the notion of chance and his desire to make his forms move in less-predictable ways led him to switch to a system of weights and balances. He created the mobile as we know it today—forms that float with random movements on a draft of air. Calder suspended objects from wooden bars, frames, or sheets of wood or metal, and hung them from the ceiling. His best-known mobiles were made with metal shapes, reminiscent of natural forms, such as leaves and fish, welded to wires and attached to one another in a series of freely moving units. Most of his mobiles are asymmetrical arrangements—diagonal lines and arcs shot off into the air, supporting large groups of shapes surprisingly balanced by only one or two other forms. He used color the same way—painting one shape a primary accent color (usually red) to visually balance a large group of black shapes. The magic of Calder's mobiles lies in their remarkable sense of balance and the playful way the forms interact in ever-changing combinations of line, shape, and color, constantly reshaping space.

Materials

For each student:

- pencil
- scissors
- copy paper (optional)
- cardboard
- one to four 12-inch wooden barbecue skewers (snip off the pointy ends with a plier cutter) or dowels (1/4- to 1/2-inch in diameter)
- 2 to 3 yards of black yarn
- 1 foot fishing line
- rulers

To share:

- compass, rulers
- white glue
- masking tape
- tempera paint
- 1/2- to 1-inch foam or flat brushes
- Styrofoam trays for mixing paint
- newspaper
- clothesline (optional)

About This Project

Making a mobile is a great way to learn about physical weights and balances, as well as visual balance in design. Like Calder, students will create hanging mobiles, with the emphasis on shape, line, color, and abstract design. They'll cut the shapes out of cardboard and compose the linear elements with black yarn and dowels. Younger students can make one-unit mobiles with a few simple hanging shapes. Older students will enjoy the challenge of making multi-unit mobiles.

Before You Begin

Prepare a few types of shapes (see page 69) and two types of units (hanging and attached shapes) for demonstration. String a clothesline for balancing long mobiles and for display. Show examples of Calder's work. Display some mobiles and demonstrate physical balance. Explain to students that mobiles are built in units. For this project, a unit consists of one or more shapes that are glued to a dowel and/or suspended with yarn. Any unit can be balanced when it's suspended, even a unit with a single heavy shape hanging near one end of the dowel. Students just have to find the balance point on the dowel (see below). The shapes also have to be balanced to hang at the correct angle, which is any position the students choose for their design. Hanging shapes can be attached to the dowel at any point. Attach glued shapes at the ends of the dowel.

Balancing Act

To demonstrate balance, hang a metal spoon near the end of a dowel. Tie a piece of yarn to the dowel and slide it along the dowel until you find the balance point (very close to the spoon). This is an example of *asymmetrical balance*—the balance point is off-center. When all the weights are evenly distributed, the balance point is at the center of the dowel and the unit is *symmetrically balanced* (like a scale). To demonstrate this, hang a spoon at the center of the dowel or two shapes of equal weight an equal distance from the center.

Students also can suspend units that are slightly off-balance and let the dowel tilt a bit diagonally. Diagonals make the overall design more dynamic. But if the dowel tilts too much, the pieces will slide to one side and the unit will collapse.

Show students how to estimate the balance point by holding the unit loosely in the air.

Design and Paint the Shapes

Every mobile has a central theme (the way it looks when it's not in motion). Students can design the theme in several ways. They can make a pencil sketch of a design and then cut the shapes, or they can make eight to 12 shapes first and either:

- Lay out the dowels and shapes on their desk (for long multi-unit mobiles, lay them out on the floor on top of newspaper) and make a quick sketch of the layout for reference.

- Design spontaneously as they attach shapes. Remind students that they'll need to vary heights and spaces between forms to allow the shapes to move freely. They should include one or two dominant shapes to add interest and variety to the design (they can also achieve this with color).

1. Have students draw the shapes on cardboard and cut them out. Shapes can be irregular and/or geometric, ranging in size from two to six inches. They can be different, repetitive, or similar but different in size.

   - **Open shapes:** Cut out the center of a shape (cut into the form, then seal the cut with white glue or masking tape). Open shapes will allow the students to add large shapes without a lot of weight.

   - **Spirals:** Begin by cutting a circular shape. Then make a diagonal cut 1/2 inch into the circle and keep cutting around the form (maintaining the 1/2-inch width) to the center. Pop out the center and pull the spiral apart. These curvilinear, 3-D forms will add contrast to a design consisting of mostly flat shapes. The weight will vary, depending on the size of the circular shape.

   - **Three-dimensional sphere:** Intersect two same-size circles. Cut notches (as wide as the thickness of the cardboard) up to the halfway point in both pieces. Slide one inside the other. Adjust the fit and glue them together. Other shapes can be intersected the same way. These heavier forms will add weight to a small or large shape.

2. Remind students to keep their color schemes simple. Suggest that they use two or three colors and make one the accent color. They can paint the shapes the same or different colors on each side. Have them apply a few coats of paint to get a rich, smooth finish—don't forget to paint the edges.

3. Have students paint the dowels black (including the tips) with two coats of paint. If students are attaching shapes to the dowel, have them glue the shapes first before painting. Paint the section of the dowel behind the shape the same color as the shape and paint the rest of the dowel black.

Tip

If the students are designing multi-unit mobiles spontaneously, they should make 8 to 12 shapes so they have a good selection.

Balance and Assemble Shapes and Units

Single-Unit Mobile:

1. To balance a shape, students should decide how they want to position each shape; they can hang it vertically, diagonally, etc. Geometric shapes are easy to balance—simply locate its center. Irregular shapes are a little trickier. Have the students hold the shape loosely between the thumb and forefinger and balance it in the air. Poke a small hole at the balance point with the compass point (about 1/4 inch from the edge). Hang the shape from a piece of fishing line to test its balance. If the shape isn't hanging at the desired angle, rebalance and poke another small hole. Once it's balanced correctly, twist a pencil inside the hole to widen it for the yarn.

2. Have students cut the yarn in varying lengths for each shape. Pull the yarn through the shape's hole and tie a double knot.

3. Tie all the shapes tightly to the dowel with a double knot and glue the knots to the dowel.

4. To balance the unit (the mobile), students can estimate the balance point by holding the dowel loosely between the thumb and forefinger. Mark the spot with a pencil.

5. Cut the suspender (a piece of yarn about 2- to 2 1/2-feet long) to hang the mobile. Tie the yarn at the balance point with a single knot. Suspend the mobile to test its balance. If the mobile isn't balanced, slide the suspender along the dowel to find its balance point, then tie a double knot and glue it to the dowel.

6. Trim any excess yarn around the all knots. The mobile is ready to hang.

Multi-Unit Mobile:

Multi-unit mobiles are assembled from the bottom unit up. Students will have to balance the bottom unit before attaching it to the one above. Once two units are attached, the combined unit has to be balanced before attaching it to the next one. Finally, students will have to find the balance point on the top dowel, which supports everything, to suspend the mobile. As the mobile gets longer, students will probably need to lay it on the floor (on newspaper), then suspend it from a clothesline to balance it.

Tip

To balance a unit or finished mobile, you have to slide the suspender around the dowel to find the balance point. Try one of these tips:
● Hold the suspender (yarn) in the air (or have a partner do it).
● Tape a ruler to the edge of the desk and tie the yarn to it. (Wind the yarn around the ruler to shorten it if necessary.)
● Tie the mobile to a clothesline with a single knot.

March

Project 2: Weather Vane

Create a traditional or original moveable weather vane.

Sessions: 3–4

Curriculum Connections: Science, Social Studies

Techniques: Drawing, painting, cutting

Art Objective: Sculpture

Visual Vocabulary: Socket, balance, faux finish, silhouette, profile

Art References: Folk Art: weather vanes; **Historic Vanes:** Shem Drowne's grasshopper on Boston's Faneuil Hall, Thomas Jefferson's designs for Monticello and the University of Virginia, George Washington's design for Mount Vernon, Paul Revere's wooden codfish for his shop in Boston

Art Talk

Before the invention of the barometer, weather vanes helped people predict weather by indicating the direction of the winds. The oldest documented weather vane, made in about 48 B.C., was a bronze figure of the Greek sea god Triton that swirled above the Tower of the Winds in Athens. Metal replicas of heraldic banners topped medieval castles; European tradesmen used them to advertise their businesses. Vanes were mounted on church spires and tall public buildings, where they were visible to all. Weather vanes were especially useful to farmers, who lived in towns and worked in the fields.

In rural America, farmers lived on isolated farms, and each needed his own weather vane. Necessity prompted the growth of a wonderful folk-art tradition. Vanes of every sort topped barns and farmhouses, from rustic designs whittled out of wood, to silhouetted shapes forged in iron or cut from sheet metal, to handsome gilded copper full-bodied sculptures created by professional vane makers. Early motifs followed European conventions—roosters, banners, pennants, or arrows. Mid-18th-century subjects included horses and other domestic animals, Indians, angels, and mythological figures. In the 19th century, exotic animals and industrial symbols, such as trains and fire-fighting equipment, became the trend. In the 1920s and 30s, black metal silhouette "story" vanes were manufactured as decorative items for homeowners. Though weather vanes may have lost their original function, they've never lost their aesthetic appeal.

Materials
(sculpture)

For each student:

- 18- by 24-inch tracing paper
- 18-inch square corrugated cardboard (or rigid pizza box)
- scrap cardboard
- pencil
- heavy black marker
- 1/2-pint milk carton
- 12- to 18-inch wooden dowel (3/8-inch or 1/2-inch in diameter)
- two 2 1/4-inch Styrofoam squares
- T-squares (see page 73)

To share:

- masking tape

For teacher:

- scissors
- plaster of paris (about 10 lbs for 30 students)
- measuring cup
- water
- two 9- by 12-inch sheets of tagboard
- glue gun (optional)
- paper cutter (optional)
- large cardboard box for storage (optional)

(continued on page 74)

About This Project

Students will design a weather vane, cut the shape out of cardboard, and paint it to resemble a tarnished copper or black metal vane, or a more colorful piece of art. They'll attach a socket and dowel to one side (to allow the vane to turn) and mount it on a plaster base. Encourage students to use traditional motifs or contemporary ones, such as a school bus, racing car, rocket, or action figure. Like many appealing folk-art vanes, their vanes can be realistic or stylized.

Before You Begin

Show your class pictures of different types of weather vanes. Have students bring in reference materials for their vanes (e.g., pictures of weather vanes, animals or objects, or model toys). Read and discuss Drawing (page 10).

Cut the tagboard to make eight 2- by 12-inch strips. Wrap them around a dowel to make long cylinders and glue the seams with white glue or a glue gun. (These will be cut into smaller pieces to make the sockets later.)

Make the Base (NOTE: You may want to do this yourself.)

1. Cover the work surface with newspaper and line up the milk cartons.

2. Punch a hole in the center of one Styrofoam square with the dowel. Put the other Styrofoam square on the bottom of each carton to make the base smooth.

3. Pour 1/3 cup cold water into each carton and add 2/3 cup of plaster of paris (or follow label instructions). Tamp the carton on the table a few times to release the air bubbles. Stir the mixture with the dowel, then tamp the container again.

4. As the plaster starts to set, press the Styrofoam square with the hole against the plaster and insert the dowel. Let the base harden (about half an hour).

Design the Vane and Cut the Shapes

1. Have students tape the tracing paper over the cardboard and lightly draw a rough outline of the weather vane with an unsharpened pencil. The shape should be big enough to fill the entire cardboard, touching all the edges. Narrower subjects, such as arrows or fish, won't fill the entire format but the drawing should touch the top and side edges.

2. Refine the drawing and fill in the details (see Tip, page 73).

3. Show students how to cut the shape out of the cardboard. (You might want to let them practice cutting shapes out of scrap pieces of cardboard before they start to cut their vanes. See Cutting, page 9.)

4. Have students copy the drawing to fill in the details on the cardboard. Then turn over the tracing paper and cardboard and copy the details on the other side. (See page 24 for another way to replicate the tracing paper drawing.)

5. Have students retrace the details with a black marker. When they paint the vane, the lines should show through faintly.

Balance the Vanes and Attach the Sockets

These decorative vanes don't have to catch the wind, but they will seem more authentic if they can turn. Help each child find the vane's balance point and attach the socket:

1. To locate the vane's balance point, hold the top of the vane loosely between the thumb and index finger and balance it in the air. Mark the spot with a pencil near the bottom of the figure.

2. Cut the tagboard cylinder into a socket sized to fit the vane (about 1 1/2 to 2 1/2 inches). Pinch the top of the socket together and seal it with hot or white glue. Center the socket on the vane's balance point and glue it to the vane.

Tip

Draw parallel lines for vehicles, flags, arrows, with a T-square. For wheels or other repetitive shapes, such as windows, students can use cardboard templates cut out of scrap cardboard.

Make a Cardboard T-square:
Cut two strips of corrugated cardboard 2- by 18-inch and 2- by 9-inch (you can use the end flaps of a pizza box). Overlap the center of the short strip with the long strip by about an inch. Make sure they're perpendicular to each other (the inside corners should be right angles), then staple together.

Using a Cardboard T-square:
Hook the short part (overlapped side faceup) against the left edge of the cardboard. Slide the T-square up or down to position it. Hold the shaft of the T-square down with one hand. Press the pencil point in the top inside corner and drag the pencil along the edge.

Materials (painting)

To share:

- tempera paint (primary colors plus black and white)

- wide foam or bristle brushes

- detail brushes

- water tins

- plastic bowls or tuna tins for paint

- Styrofoam tray (palette for realistic painting only)

- newspaper

- baby wipes or paper towels

For faux painting:

- cellulose sponge
- water-based copper paint
- rubber gloves

Paint the Vane

Set up different areas for different types of finishes. Cover all work surfaces with newspaper.

1. **Faux Finish:** Faux (French for "imitation") finishes simulate real surfaces or textures:

   - Mix yellow, blue, and a little white paint to make a few bowls of turquoise green for the base coat. (If the mixture is too green, add a drop of black.) Save some of the mixture to make the glaze—add it to white paint to make it a color that's a few shades lighter, then thin the mixture with a little water to make a milky consistency. Cut a sponge into 1-inch strips. Use cardboard scraps to test the glaze.

   - Have students paint the base coat on both sides of the vane, including the socket, with a wide foam or bristle brush. The detail lines should show through. When the paint is completely dry, have students go over the details with a thick black marker. (For subtler effects, use a dark gray, green, or turquoise marker.)

   - Show students how to glaze their vane. Dip the tip of the sponge into the glaze. Blot off the excess paint on a cardboard scrap. The sponge should be relatively dry to create the texture. Stamp the sponge around the vane randomly, with a quick, light touch, to create a natural effect. Let some of the base coat show through. Use smaller pieces of sponge to add copper highlights. Sponging along the top edge of the detail lines will make the details look more three-dimensional.

2. **Wrought-Iron Finish:** Have students paint the entire vane black. These vanes should have an interesting silhouette because they won't have any surface details. After the paint dries, students may want to sponge on a touch of red or copper to simulate rust.

3. **Decorative Painting:** Prepare primary colors and black and white paint for detail colors. Students can paint the background a solid color and add colorful details over it or paint several colors simultaneously.

4. **Base and Dowel:** Peel off the milk carton from the dried plaster base. Paint the dowel and base copper, black, or white, or leave the wood unpainted. Mount the vane on the dowel and turn!

April

Theme: *Spring to Life*

The cycle of life is renewed in the spring. These projects explore insect forms and the underwater world of plants and animals and the miniature world of insects.

Project 1: **Sea-Life Collage**

Create an underwater collage with colorful plants and animals.

Sessions: 2

Curriculum Connections: Science, Nature

Technique: Collage

Art Objective: Design

Visual Vocabulary: Line, shape, color, texture, pattern, contrast, emphasis, overlap, crop, symmetry, asymmetry, balance, movement, diagonal, theme, motif

Art References: Scenic murals and mosaics; underwater photography; Matisse cut-paper collages

Art Talk

Marine life was a favorite subject of the Minoans, who inhabited the island of Crete 3,500 years ago. Their fluid and rhythmic style of painting seemed to echo the floating world that inspired much of their art. The walls of their palaces were painted with landscapes and aquatic scenes. The Minoans also created a type of pottery, called the Marine Style, which they decorated with playful paintings of octopi, fish, shells, and sea plants. This style spread to the mainland, where the Mycenaeans, a pre-Greek culture, adapted it in a stiffer, more stylized form. Sea-life subjects also appeared frequently in mosaics, another ancient medium used throughout the Greco-Roman world. Aquatic plants, animals, sea monsters, and fishing and mythological scenes were perfect subjects for the decorative mosaics that adorned the bathhouses, as well as the fountains and courtyards of public buildings and private villas.

Marine subjects have always been used as decorative motifs and often appeared in still-life paintings. But the underwater seascapes, so popular in ancient times, disappeared with those civilizations. In the 20th century, the exciting art of underwater photography revealed this world again.

Materials

For each student:

- 9- by 12-inch and 12- by 18-inch tracing paper
- 12- by 18-inch drawing paper
- pencil
- scissors

To share:

- glue sticks
- hole punch
- 9- by 12-inch and 12- by 18-inch colored construction paper
- newspaper

Creature Features

Make eyes, dots, or bubbles, with a hole punch or small pieces of torn colored paper. To make stripes that fit the contour of a fish or shell, draw outlines of curved lines on the drawing paper template or use tracing paper to make a copy of the shape, then draw the curves. Use the template to cut the colored paper.

About This Project

The sea is full of creatures and plants of every size, shape, pattern, and color, making it a wonderful subject for collage. A field trip to an aquarium would be a great way to begin. Sketching from life will help students form a clear picture of an underwater environment, and they can use their sketches as reference for their collages. If such a field trip isn't possible, visit a marine Web site or show your class a film or video on the subject, and have students bring in pictures for reference. Show Matisse collages as examples of style and technique.

The students will use their reference material to draw and cut out colored paper shapes. They can create a naturalistic underwater scene, or an imaginary one filled with sea monsters and mythological sea creatures. Read and discuss Collage (page 12), Drawing (page 10), and Design (page 16). Demonstrate various techniques.

Draw the Shapes and Make the Collage

1. Have students make outline drawings of individual fish, shell, and plant shapes on drawing paper for templates or draw directly on colored construction paper. Encourage them to use contrasting colors and values (lights and darks) for a variety of shapes.

2. Have students cut and/or tear out the shapes. Remind them that they can cut or tear repetitive shapes, such as plants or schools of fish together with a few sheets of colored paper.

3. Invite students to choose a background color from 12- by 18-inch colored construction paper.

4. Have students arrange the shapes on the background into an interesting scene. They can overlap some shapes or cluster a group together and isolate others. They also can crop shapes and vary the angles and directions of the shapes to create a feeling of movement. Let them cut new shapes, eliminate others, or trade shapes with friends to improve their composition.

5. Encourage students to add bright, colorful details to create features, textures, and patterns (see "Creature Features"). Tell them to glue on small details immediately.

6. Have them glue the rest of the pieces to finish the collage, working from the top layer down.

April

Project 2: **Bug Prints**

Create bug-motif patterns and designs to print on paper and T-shirts.

Sessions: 2–3

Curriculum Connections: Science, Nature

Technique: Relief printing

Art Objectives: Design, printmaking

Visual Vocabulary: Symmetry, relief printing, engraving, brayer

Art References: Relief Prints: Albrecht Dürer, Paul Gauguin, Emile Nolde, Edvard Munch, German Expressionists, José Guadaloupe Posada, Leonard Baskin, Barry Moser, Japanese color woodcuts, Picasso (linoleum cuts); **Insect Illustrations and Motifs:** Textile and jewelry designs, Egyptian scarabs, nature books (Utamaro's *Insects*), Alain Séguy, M.C. Escher

Art Talk

Relief printing is the oldest form of printing. The technique originated in China in the 9th century, where woodblocks (the traditional medium) were first used for stamping designs on textiles. Woodblock printing also was the earliest method for printing money, newspapers, illustrated books, and multiple works of art. The process is simple and direct. Lines or shapes that aren't going to be printed are cut away from the block's surface. The part that remains, which is raised (or stands in "relief"), is inked and printed.

Contemporary artists make relief prints in all kinds of styles, using traditional or new materials, such as cardboard, plastic, metal, or Styrofoam. Any surface that can be incised or raised by adding smooth or textured materials can be used to make relief prints.

Insects are perfect subjects for relief printing. Their symmetrical, segmented bodies and simple shapes are easy to draw, cut out, or engrave, and arrange into bold patterns and designs. Their forms, colors, and decorative patterns have always inspired artists and designers. Insect motifs have long appeared on textiles, jewelry, coins and crests. The scarab beetle, which was associated with the sun god, was a favorite Egyptian motif. It was used for seals, amulets, ornaments, and hieroglyphics. The Mayans also used insect forms in their alphabet. Twentieth-century artists Alain Séguy and M.C. Escher created many inventive patterns using insect motifs.

Materials
(for drawings and plates)

For each student:

- pencil
- marker
- 9- by 12-inch tracing paper
- scissors
- two 5- by 7-inch Styrofoam trays (or precut foam board plates)
- graph paper (optional)
- wooden stylus (optional)

To share:

- white glue
- masking tape
- toothpicks

(continued on page 80)

About This Project

Most kids are fascinated by bugs. They'll enjoy exploring different aspects of pattern and design using insect motifs. This project also will make a wonderful adjunct to a unit on insects or symmetry.

Students will make their printing plates out of Styrofoam. They should make two types of plates—engraved plates and raised-shape plates (made with cut-out Styrofoam shapes glued to a backing). These techniques will produce different effects and give students a better understanding of the relief-printing process.

Students can wash and reuse the same plate to make prints in different colors or make multiple prints of the same plate on one sheet of paper. For a grand finale, they can print their plates on T-shirts. They can also use them to make stamps, greeting cards, calendars, or book illustrations. To make a class book of insects, have each student make an additional print.

Before You Begin

Here's a dramatic way to demonstrate symmetry: Draw a ladybug, fold it in half, and hold a mirror perpendicular to the fold. Show students examples of relief prints. Prepare or have students bring in pictures of bugs that clearly define their basic shapes. (The *National Audubon Society Field Guide to North American Insects and Spiders* index contains excellent examples of silhouetted insect shapes.) If you're making plates from the inexpensive Styrofoam trays, cut off the edges on a paper cutter, or have students cut them off with scissors. You may want to cut some 9- by 12-inch paper in half for printing single plates. Invite a parent or other volunteer to assist with the printing process (especially with younger children).

Make the Drawings

FOR RAISED-SHAPE PLATES: The shapes will print the color of the ink. The background will be the color of the paper. Students also can engrave lines into the raised shapes.

1. Tell students to make outline drawings of different bug shapes, about 2 to 3 inches, on tracing paper. (A top view is best.) They can put graph paper under the tracing paper to help with symmetry. They should outline legs (not too skinny or they might break off when cut). Or they can draw the body and add toothpicks to indicate legs or antennae when preparing the plate.

2. Before students cut their drawings, they should fold each drawing in half and pick the side that

looks best. Then, cut the folded drawing along lines to make a template. (This will make the shape perfectly symmetrical.) Open it up and draw the details.

FOR ENGRAVED PLATES: The background will print the color of the ink. The lines, which are below the surface, will be the color of the paper.

1. Have students create a format on tracing paper by tracing around the Styrofoam plate.

2. They can create a composition by sketching a few types of bugs in various shapes and sizes (seen from any angle). They can also create a pattern by tracing around the cut-out template and alternately turning it upside down or sideways. Draw the details.

Prepare the Plates

FOR RAISED-SHAPE PLATES: Relief plates print in reverse, so all drawings will have to be turned over when they're transferred to the plates. (This step isn't critical with symmetrical subjects, but it will be important if students want to write their names on the plates.) Remind students that every indentation on the plate will show up on the print. The surface should be smooth and handled carefully.

1. Help students place their bug templates on a piece of Styrofoam. They can either trace around it with a marker or tape it to the plate and cut it out.

2. Glue each shape to a Styrofoam backing with white glue. (The backing should be a little bigger than the bug.) If they're using toothpicks, add glue, stick the toothpicks into the body, and then press them on the backing. The glue will take a few minutes to dry. Students can also glue a few bug shapes to a larger piece of Styrofoam backing.

3. Tell students to copy bug details from the drawing onto the Styrofoam with a marker. (Or use the transfer technique for Engraved Plates, next page.)

4. Engrave the details by dragging the stylus (or pencil) along the lines. Tell students to press hard. Use the flat end of the stylus to create thick lines and fat dots (great for segment divisions and ladybug dots). Use the pointy side to make thin lines and dots (great for details and texture).

Tip

Students shouldn't make lines too close together; they won't hold up when the plate is engraved.

Materials
(for printing)

To share:

- water-based printing ink in large tubes or cans (or tempera paint)
- 2-inch and/or 4-inch brayers (rubber rollers with handles) for each color (or foam brushes)
- 9- by 12-inch Styrofoam tray for each inker
- wooden spoons (or clean brayers) for each printer
- copy paper
- 9- by 12-inch construction or other printing paper
- newspaper
- baby wipes (or paper towels and water)
- spatulas for each can of ink (optional)

For teacher:

- clotheslines and clothespins (optional)

FOR ENGRAVED PLATES: Have students transfer their drawings to the plates by placing them reversed on the Styrofoam. They can use one of these techniques:

- Poke dots along the lines with the pointy side of the stylus, then remove the template. Connect the dots to engrave the plate.

- Drag the stylus along the lines of the drawing. (The paper will tear but that's okay.) Students may have to go over the lines again to make them deeper after removing the paper.

- Use a marker and copy the drawing onto the Styrofoam. They can then engrave the design with the pencil or stylus. Add texture to the background or shapes using lines or dots.

Make the Prints

Printing is a multistep process that's best done in an organized fashion. The first step is to set up different stations for inking, paper distribution, printing, cleaning, and drying. The idea is to keep the wet processes separate from the dry ones. You can either have one large centralized area in which the different stations are arranged in assembly-line fashion, or you can divide the class into small groups of six students. Have the students in each group push their desks together and set up each desk as a different station:

STATION 1: INKING THE PLATES. Consider setting up separate stations for each color. If possible, staff this station with parent volunteers. Cover all surface with newspapers and provide more newspapers, ink, inking trays, and brayers for each color (or bowls of paint and foam brushes), and baby wipes or paper towels.

STATION 2: PAPER SELECTION AND DISTRIBUTION.

STATION 3: PRINTING THE PLATES. Cover the work surface with newspaper and stock with a wooden spoon or clean brayer and baby wipes and paper towels.

STATION 4: DRYING THE PRINTS. Any clean flat surface or a clothesline stretched across the room.

STATION 5: CLEANING THE PLATES. Stock this area with newspaper, baby wipes, or water and paper towels.

1. **Inking the plates:** Spread a thick line of ink across the top of the inking tray. Roll a film of ink across the tray with the brayer a few times and coat the brayer evenly with a moderate amount of ink. The ink should feel tacky. Roll the ink across the plate with a few strokes,

overlapping each new pass until the plate is fully covered. The ink should have the same sheen all over the plate. Roll more ink over spotty areas (or coat the plate with tempera paint using a foam brush the same way). Put each inked plate face-up on a clean sheet of newspaper and discard the used paper. Use a baby wipe or damp paper towel to wipe off excess ink on the backing of raised-shape plates.

2. **Paper selection:** Have students select a paper and bring it to the printing station.

3. **Printing (or "pulling" the print):** Place the paper over the plate or plates. Try to center the paper over the plate(s). Rub the back of the paper with the back of the spoon or clean brayer several times. Apply pressure. Cover every inch to make a good impression. Pull the paper off slowly and evenly. If necessary, hold down the corner of the plate with a finger or the shaft of the spoon.

4. **Drying the prints:** A student with clean hands should bring the print to the drying station. Hang the print from the clothesline with clothespins or spread them out on a clean surface.

   Another child should handle the inky plate. To make extra prints in the same color, return the plate to the inking station. To print the plate in another color, bring the plate to the cleaning station first.

5. **Cleaning the plates:** Wash the plates with water or clean with a baby wipe. Store the plates in plastic sandwich bags.

Print T-shirts

1. You may want to offer students the option of printing on T-shirts. The inking process is the same, but you'll need an opaque fabric ink. Read the label for instructions. Some brands of ink may work better with foam brushes than brayers; try both.

2. To print, place the shirt printing side up over a cushion of folded newspapers on a clean table. (Make sure to smooth out the wrinkles.) Put the inked plate (or plates) facedown on the shirt. Once the plate is on the shirt, don't move anything. Make a fist and rub the back of the plate hard without moving it. Peel off the plate slowly. Put the shirt on a hanger to dry.

Note

The first print is usually a "proof" to determine if corrections to the plate are needed. Proofs can be made on copy paper or construction paper. If the engraved lines fill with ink or if the ink prints too thickly, try working the ink off the brayer by rolling it on the inking tray or re-engravng the lines. If the coverage is uneven or too thin, it's either an inking or printing problem. Use more ink and roll it across the plate more carefully, or rub the back of the paper more evenly and with more pressure.

May

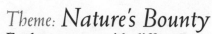
Theme: ***Nature's Bounty***
Explore nature with different media—drawing, collage, and painting.

Project 1: **Still Life**
Draw, paint, and make a collage of a still life composed of natural objects.

Sessions: 2–3

Curriculum Connection: Nature

Techniques: Collage, painting

Art Objectives: Design, composition

Visual Vocabulary: Still life, collage, form, background elements

Art References: Dutch and Flemish still lifes, Chardin, Cotán, Cézanne, Van Gogh, Matisse, Harnett, Picasso, Braque, Magritte, Duchamp, Ernst, Cornell, Stuart Davis, Jasper Johns, Thiebald, Warhol, Koons

Art Talk

Still lifes had appeared in Western art in ancient wall paintings and mosaics, or as elements in grand paintings with classical, historical, and biblical themes created for princes and popes. But inanimate objects weren't considered important enough to be painted as independent subjects until changing conditions in 17th-century Holland created a new class of art patrons—prosperous traders and merchants—who wanted small, secular paintings to decorate their homes and shops. Dutch and Flemish painting workshops met the demand with popular new themes—landscapes, "genre" paintings (scenes of everyday life), and still lifes.

Classical still-life themes emerged: *vanitas* paintings (skull, hour glass, and other symbols of fleeting time), flower arrangements, lavish banquet tables, fruit baskets, wine, and bread. Objects were meticulously painted and set against dark backgrounds to emphasize their gleaming forms.

In the mid-19th century, French painter Paul Cézanne began to explore the still life with a fresh eye and the modern still life was born. He replaced the plain dark background with shapes and colors and used broad strokes of color instead of high contrast to define forms and planes. He tilted the table top and played with perspective, painting objects from different points of view. Later, artists used the still life to develop other radical concepts—abstraction, fauvism, cubism, collage, surrealism, dada, pop, and installation art. The still life, once considered a minor art form, became the catalyst for many great and outrageous innovations of modern art.

About This Project

Students will explore traditional still-life themes with drawings, collage, and paintings. Each medium will produce different results and allow them to explore the subject in-depth. Start with thumbnail sketches, make the collage, and then move on to painting. Cutting shapes out of paper will help students see the objects as bold, simple forms. The colored backgrounds will make them more aware of space within the format. Once they get the idea, they'll be able to compose a better painting.

Before You Begin

Read and discuss Drawing (page 10), Composition (page 16), Collage (page 12), and Gluing techniques (page 8). See "Leaf-Design Collage" (page 33) for more tips. If possible, have your class do "Exciting Experiments with Color" (page 26) before they begin painting. Show samples of still-life paintings and collages.

Collect an assortment of traditional still-life objects (e.g., baskets, bottles, pottery, vase of flowers). Select and arrange the objects or invite students to do it. Consider how the objects relate to one another in terms of size, shape, color, and texture. You can use a cardboard box to elevate some objects. Drape a cloth over it or incorporate it into the design.

For large classes, divide students into groups and set up different still-life arrangements. If possible, place each still life in front of a solid background and arrange the desks around it in a semicircle.

Draw the Still Life and Make the Collage

1. Distribute the copy paper and cardboard templates. Have students trace around the templates to make a few thumbnail formats, then sketch some vertical and horizontal layouts. They can draw the entire still life or crop tightly around it, zoom in on a detail, or add elements to the background to pull the design together. Remind students that the objects should relate to one another, the space around them, and the borders of the format.

2. Have students choose the best layout and make an outline drawing of the still life on the larger drawing paper.

Materials

For each student:

- pencil
- 2 1/4- by 3 1/2-inch cardboard template
- copy paper
- 12- by 18-inch sturdy drawing paper
- scissors
- Styrofoam tray (palette)

To share:

- still-life objects
- 14- by 17-inch tracing paper
- 9- by 12-inch and 12- by 18-inch colored construction paper
- glue sticks
- paint
- tins for paint and water
- mixing sticks
- a variety of brushes
- newspaper
- baby wipes or paper towels and water

For teacher:

- small boxes
- cloth

Tip

MAKE A
BOUQUET:
Tear multi-
colored petals
out of construc-
tion paper.

MAKE A ROSE:
Cut the shape
and glue a
cutout spiral in
a different color
on top.

MAKE A DAISY:
Accordion-fold
the paper, draw
half of the petal
opposite the
fold, and cut a
bunch of sym-
metrical petals
at the same
time.

MAKE SOME
TULIPS:
Make templates
for a tulip and a
stem and cut
them out in
multiples.

3. Tell students to make collage templates by drawing each object separately on tracing paper. Have them fill in the lines of objects overlapped by other objects to make complete shapes. Outline the details, then cut out the templates.

4. Have students choose colored paper for their shapes and pick a background color that will work well with the other colors.

5. Using the templates, students can cut or tear out the shapes from the colored paper. Cut the details with the same templates. (Students can also cut or tear small shapes directly from the colored paper.) They should glue small details to shapes as soon as they're cut.

6. Have students arrange the shapes on the background. Remind them that the composition should fill the format. If necessary, they can subtract shapes, recut them, cut new ones, or add stripes or other patterns or shapes to the background to improve the design.

7. Once the collage is assembled, tell students to leave everything in place and glue on the pieces, working from the top layer down.

Create the Painting

1. Have students make a full-size drawing on 12- by 18-inch drawing paper. They can refer to their collage sketch for the layout, or if they're painting a different still life, make new thumbnail sketches.

2. Distribute paint supplies. Before students begin to paint, demonstrate different techniques to create different effects:

- Create hard edges by painting over or next to dry edges.

- Soften edges by blending wet paint into wet paint.

- Use light and dark tones or colors to create contrast. Blend contrasting tones around the edge of an object to model the form.

- Create a "painterly" effect by using thicker paint and mixing color into color on the paper.

- Use a thin wash to create a watercolor effect and thicker paint to create flat colors.

- Create texture with a stiff brush and heavy strokes of paint.

3. Have students paint the still life.

May

Project 2: Guess What? Nature Book

Draw natural objects and assemble them into a book of surprises.

Sessions: 1–2

Curriculum Connections: Science, Nature

Techniques: Drawing, bookmaking

Art Objectives: Observation, illustration

Visual Vocabulary: Herbals, botanicals, nature illustration; lines, shape, form, color, texture, shading, contour, edges

Art References: Nature books, prints, and artists: Redouté (botanicals), Audubon (birds), Utamaro (insects)

Art Talk

Although *herbals* (illustrated books that describe medicinal plants) have been produced for at least 2,000 years, the art of nature illustration really began in Europe in the 16th century, as the field of modern science was beginning to develop. Exploratory expeditions around the globe brought back exciting specimens of plants, animals, insects, shells, and seeds. This sparked a widespread fascination with the natural world that would last for centuries.

Illustrations for early mass-produced nature books were reprinted from a common pool of woodblocks, but the growing number of new scientific texts required new illustrations. Artists were commissioned to make scientifically accurate drawings, and drawing directly from nature became the standard.

Some of the most famous *botanicals* (books illustrating any type of plant) are reproductions of folios of drawings commissioned by royal and aristocratic patrons who wanted to record their plant collections. Artists drew from specimens, worked in hot houses and gardens, or traveled the globe to capture plants and animals in their natural habitats. Although the drawings (usually water color paintings) had to be precise, they were also very beautiful, and each artist developed a distinctive style. Reproduced as black-and-white woodcuts, etchings or engravings, the books were often hand-colored by women and children. Although photographers now produce the majority of work and illustrators often use photos for reference, many artists continue to produce nature illustrations by drawing directly from nature.

Materials

For each student:

- 12- by 6-inch black construction paper
- 6 sheets of 11- by 5 1/2-inch opaque drawing paper
- pencils
- pointy scissors (5-inch detail scissors work best)

To share:

- fruits, vegetables, shells, flowers (real or synthetic)
- colored markers, crayons, pencils, or paint
- small cardboard templates cut in different geometric shapes (cut 1 1/2- to 1 3/4-inch squares and circles, and triangles with two 2-inch sides)
- 2 large paper clips

For teacher:

- knife
- long-reach stapler
- paper cutter

About This Project

Students will create their own book of nature illustrations with a modern twist. They'll make four colored drawings of different natural objects on the right side of their paper. When they fold the paper and assemble the pages into a book, a blank page will appear in front of each drawing. The students will cut a small window in the center of each page to expose a small section of the object. Their friends will have to guess the object before turning the page to see the whole illustration.

Drawing real or synthetic fruit, vegetables, shells, and flowers from life will also help sharpen student's observational skills. If necessary, students also can draw from photographs. Seed and bulb catalogs are a good resource.

Before You Begin

Ask students to bring a natural object (or photographs) to class. Cut some fruits and vegetables in half. Cross sections of apples, oranges, tomatoes, and peppers will make interesting drawings, too. Read and discuss drawing (page 10) and cutting techniques (page 9). Prepare materials and make a sample book.

Make the Drawings

1. Give each student five sheets of precut drawing paper (one for practice). Have them fold each sheet in half, making sure the edges meet.

2. Have students start with a practice drawing. Tell them all the drawings must be done on the right side of the inside fold (the righthand page). Each object should fill the page. If students are drawing small or narrow objects, such as string beans or peas, they should draw a bunch of the objects together to fill the page.

3. Before students begin drawing, let them handle their object to become more familiar with its shape and texture. Next, have them place the object at the far end of their desk and examine it carefully. Then have them make an outline drawing of the object. Tell them to outline all the details as well (e.g., seeds, core, etc.) but not to shade anything with the pencil.

4. Have students color their drawings. Let them experiment first on the practice drawing. They should color the entire object with the lightest color first, then add the middle tones and darker colors to create texture and model the form. They can use little spots of colors, hatching (fine lines), or broad strokes that follow the contour of the form. They also can outline the shape with black or colored markers. After students finish each drawing, they should exchange objects.

Assemble the Book

1. Have students fold the black cover paper in half, making sure all the edges meet.

2. Show them how to lay the open pages on top of one another in an alternating fashion. Place the first picture face up, then the second one above it facedown (the facedown drawing will now be on the left). The second picture will become the cover picture, so students should pick their best drawing for this. Place the third picture face-up, and the last one facedown again.

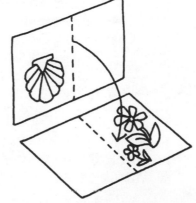

3. Refold the pages together and center them inside the cover. When you flip through the book, a blank page should appear in front of each drawing, and all the drawings should be on the right-hand pages.

4. Help students hold the pages and cover together (use paper clips if necessary). Open the book and turn it over so that the cover is on top. Staple along the fold with a long-reach stapler (set at 6 inches).

Tip

If you're using a standard stapler, place a sheet of Styrofoam under the book, open up the stapler, and staple along the fold. The staples will go through the pages but will remain open. The students can press the staples closed with a plastic knife.

Cut the Windows

1. Have students choose a cardboard template for their windows. They can cut the same or a different shape on each blank page. Have them try out these techniques a few times on a practice sheet or scrap paper before cutting the actual pages:
   - Trace around the template with a pencil to outline the shape.

- Pierce the center of the shape with the point of a scissors. For squares and triangles, cut diagonal lines from the center to the corners. (Cut past the corner a bit so the scissors can turn without ripping the paper.) For circles, cut a line from the center then trim along the outline.

2. To cut out the windows in the book, students should center the template on each blank page, except the first one, and outline the shape.

3. Have the students fold back all the book pages except for the second blank page. Have them cut out the window on this page. Repeat this step for the third and fourth blank pages.

4. For the cover and first-page window, have students center the template on the cover and trace around it. Then have them fold both the cover and the first blank page together and fold the rest of the pages back. Show students how to pierce the center of both pages and cut them together. The first drawing will show through the cover.

Note

If students want to add more pages to their books, they should do so in multiples of two to provide for window pages.

June

Theme: *Remember Me*

The heat is on and everyone is thinking about vacation. These projects will help students remember their classmates through the summer break, and for years to come.

Project 1: **Autograph Album**

Create an autograph album. Design the cover and a personal logo stamp.

Sessions: 2–3

Curriculum Connections: Poetry, penmanship

Techniques: Printmaking, bookmaking, collage

Art Objectives: Logo, book design

Visual Vocabulary: Logo, monogram, trademark, engrave

Art References: Corporate logos, trademarks, monograms; **Album Poetry:** *Dated Till Niagara Falls* and *Remember Me When You See This* by Lillian Morrison

Art Talk

The modern autograph album dates to the 16th century, when young German travelers making the grand tour of Europe brought albums along to record the flattering comments of prominent people and new acquaintances. Called *Alba Amicorum* (friendship albums), these small books served as proof of a successful journey.

The fad spread throughout Europe. At some point, the friendship album made its way across the Atlantic. American school students were soon inscribing them with their own brand of flattery: "Roses are red/ Violets are blue/God made me pretty/What happened to you?" and dating them with one-liners like "till the kitchen sinks."

In Japan, the traveler's autograph album lives on in its most elegant form. At Shinto shrines and Buddhist temples, a monk trained in the art of calligraphy will inscribe visitors' albums with the temple's *hanko*, or seal, and sometimes add decorative seal stamps of traditional motifs, such as lotus blossoms or a chrysanthemum (the emperor's emblem). Students can get ideas for their seal designs from logos and trademarks they see every day.

Materials

For each student:

- 9- by 12-inch tracing paper
- scrap paper
- pencil
- scissors
- small pieces of Styrofoam
- 18 sheets of 11- by 4 1/4-inch white or colored copy paper
- 12- by 4 1/2-inch colored tagboard or construction paper
- 2 large paper clips
- wooden stylus

To share:

- white glue and glue sticks
- 1 1/2- to 2 1/2-inch cardboard templates cut into squares, circles, triangles, rectangles
- stamp pads (or sponges, tempera paint, and Styrofoam trays)

For teacher:

- long-reach stapler
- paper cutter

About This Project

For this project, students will create their own autograph album, design a cover and a logo stamp, which they will make with Styrofoam. Then they will inscribe their friends' albums with a poem or message and stamp it with their logo.

Before You Begin

Discuss logo design and show students examples of corporate logos, trademarks, and monograms. Tell students that they will be making a stamp with their own logo—it can be a monogram made by combining initials in an interesting way or a logo with a pictorial design. Make a sample stamp and autograph book to show students.

Design and Make the Stamp

1. Have students choose a cardboard template and trace around the shape to create a stamp format on tracing paper. Then have them trade with their classmates and create a few more formats with different shapes.

2. Encourage students to create a different logo design in each format. Students can use their initials (drawn freehand or on a computer). They can also draw decorative borders, such as zigzags or scallops, or reshape the format into flowers, fish, or another shape.

3. Let students select their favorite logo design. Then, have them turn over the drawing (remember, stamps print in reverse!), place it on a piece of Styrofoam, and cut out the stamp format. Students will need to cut two formats for raised stamps; one will be used for the backing.

4. Show students how to transfer their designs to the Styrofoam. Place the tracing over the Styrofoam. Make sure it's reversed.
   - ENGRAVED STAMPS (the background prints; engraved lines drop out): Drag the stylus or pencil along the lines, tearing through the tracing paper; or poke dots through the paper along the lines, then remove the paper and connect the dots with the stylus. Push hard to make a deep indentation in the Styrofoam.

   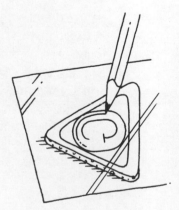

   - RAISED STAMPS (cutout letters or shapes print; background drops out):

Make a copy of the letters on another piece of tracing paper for reference. Hold or tape the original tracing (reversed!) on the Styrofoam format and cut out the letters or shapes. Arrange the cutouts on the backing piece and glue. (Refer to the copy drawing [reversed] to be sure the letters are assembled correctly.) Add engraved lines or dots if desired.

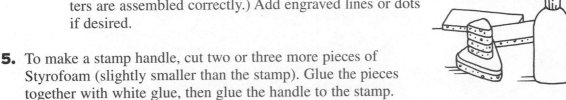

5. To make a stamp handle, cut two or three more pieces of Styrofoam (slightly smaller than the stamp). Glue the pieces together with white glue, then glue the handle to the stamp.

Assemble the Album and Design the Cover

1. Distribute the paper for the album pages. Have students stack a few blank sheets together at a time and fold them in half. Make sure all the edges line up neatly. Have them score the pages along the fold with their thumbnails.

2. Tell students to fold the tagboard in half for the cover, making sure the edges line up. Center the folded pages inside the cover and hold them in place with paper clips.

3. Have students open their albums and turn them over so that the cover is on top. Help them staple their books along the fold. Set the long-reach stapler to 6 inches. (If you're using a standard stapler, see Tip, page 87.)

4. Have students design their album cover. They can make a collage or photomontage (see page 92), add a title and picture, or stamp it with their logo.

Stamp and Sign the Albums

1. Buy commercial stamp pads or make your own with a sponge and tempera paint (for bolder prints). Pour the paint on a dampened sponge and rub it around. Refill as necessary.

2. Have students select one stamp color. Practice on scrap paper before stamping the albums. To change the color, remove the ink or paint with water or a baby wipe and dry. Stamps can be reused.

3. Have students stamp their logos on the righthand page. After the ink dries, students can write their message.

June

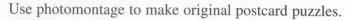

Project 2: **Fun-in-the-Sun Postcard Puzzles**

Use photomontage to make original postcard puzzles.

Session: 1

Curriculum Connection: Social Studies

Technique: Photomontage

Art Objective: Design

Visual Vocabulary: Photomontage, collage, juxtaposition, proportion

Art References: Hannah Hoch, Marcel Duchamp, Max Ernst, Joseph Cornell, David Hockney, Robert Rauschenberg, Romare Beardon; illustration and advertisements

This project combines postcards, jigsaw puzzles, and photomontage. In 1869, the Austrian government issued the first postal card. The idea spread like wildfire across Europe. In 1873, the U.S. issued its first postal card, imprinted with the image of Liberty decked out in a crown of leaves. The price: one cent. Soon picture postcards made their debut, creating a new market for artists and photographers. Sending and collecting postcards became the craze.

The first jigsaw puzzles actually were maps mounted on wood and cut with a jig saw. They originated in England during the 18th century, where they were used to teach geography. Eventually, jigsaw puzzles also were made with pictures.

Photomontage is a type of collage made primarily with photographic images. The technique developed in Germany (*montage* is German for "assembly") after World War I. Artists such as Hannah Hoch first used photomontage to satirize the popular hobby of gluing together sentimental or decorative cutouts. Dadaists and surrealists (e.g., Duchamp, Ernst) found the disorderly nature of montage a perfect medium for satirizing art and society with witty combinations of incongruous, unrelated, and out-of-scale images. Before World War II, German artists began using photomontage as a powerful expression of political protest. The technique has since been widely adopted by fine and commercial artists and filmmakers.

About This Project

The postcard puzzle is quick, easy, and fun to make. Each child will create a photomontage on card stock or cardboard and paste a puzzle template on the back. The theme is summer vacation—places students have been to or would like to visit. Images can be humorous, picturesque, surreal, or fantastic (e.g., a trip to outer space or back in time, a fantasy island, a jungle excursion). Photomontage lends itself to the odd juxtapositions of images, so students can get very creative and use any type of imagery that gets their message across. They can scan or photocopy the original and send messages to all their friends during summer vacation.

Before You Begin

Show samples of interesting vintage postcards, montages, and collages. Ask students to collect images for their postcards. Remind them that their pictures have to fit a 5- by 7-inch format. Fragments or combinations of small pictures will work best. Family pictures can be copied and then cut up. Ask students to cut their pictures at home so they'll have time to design and make more postcards in class. Provide extra montage materials and copy the puzzle template.

Make the Postcard Montages

1. Distribute the puzzle templates and have students trim around the borders. Collect and put the templates aside.

2. If children haven't cut their montage materials at home, have them do it in class. They should prepare a lot of different images. Let them trade with one another, too. They can

- cut up and use parts of family pictures (or copies) and printed materials (pictures of places, animals, vehicles, architecture, food, etc.).

- make a computer printout of the name of a location in large block letters, or cut block letters out of colored paper and fill them with montages (like travel postcards from the 1940s and 1950s).

Materials

For each student:

- Puzzle template (page 95)

- 5- by 7-inch tagboard or card stock

- scissors

To share:

- montage materials (photos, magazines, travel brochures, etc.)

- colored construction paper

- glue sticks

- markers

3. Tell students to select and arrange their images on the tagboard format. They can put faces on different bodies or combine things that are totally out of scale or context. They can restrict their designs to pictures or they can incorporate other materials. For example:

- cover the background with colored paper or use the colored paper behind pictures to make certain areas stand out.

- add cut or torn bits of colored paper.

- use letters as a graphic device, use place names or other words.

- outline shapes with a marker pen.

4. After they've arranged their designs, have students leave all the pieces in place. Then they can glue the pieces from the top layer down with glue sticks.

5. Have students coat the back of the puzzle template with a glue stick. Have them place the back of the postcard on top of the template and carefully line up the corners. Turn over the card and smooth out the template, working from the center out.

Note

Remind students to have their postcards weighed before mailing.

Summer Fun

During the summer, students can:

- duplicate the front and back to make more puzzle postcards.

- write a message and address the card (over the jigsaw outlines) and mail the postcard. Their friends can cut up the postcard to make the puzzle.

- cut the puzzles apart and mail the pieces in an envelope. When their friends assemble the puzzle, they'll get the message.

- cut the puzzle apart and keep it for their own enjoyment.

Puzzle Template

We Did It!

P.S. 217—2nd grade

P.S. 217—3rd grade

P.S. 207—2nd grade

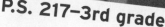